Professor Manlio Simonetti teach[...] the University of Rome and at the 'Augustinianum', the Patristic Institute in Rome.

Fr John A. Hughes is Chaplain at St Andrew's College, Glasgow.

Dr Anders Bergquist is Director of Studies and a Tutor at Westcott House, Cambridge.

Dr Markus Bockmuehl is a University Lecturer in Divinity and a Fellow and Tutor at Fitzwilliam College, Cambridge.

Dr William Horbury is a University Lecturer in Divinity and a Fellow of Corpus Christi College, Cambridge.

BIBLICAL INTERPRETATION
IN THE EARLY CHURCH

BIBLICAL INTERPRETATION IN THE EARLY CHURCH

An Historical Introduction to Patristic Exegesis

Manlio Simonetti

Translator
John A. Hughes

Editors
Anders Bergquist and Markus Bockmuehl

Consultant Editor
William Horbury

T&T CLARK
EDINBURGH

T&T CLARK LTD
59 GEORGE STREET
EDINBURGH EH2 2LQ
SCOTLAND

First Published 1994

ISBN 0 567 09557 6 (HB)
ISBN 0 567 29249 5 (PB)

British Library Cataloguing-in-Publication Data
A catalogue record for this book
is available from the British Library

Typeset by Trinity Typesetting, Edinburgh
Printed and bound in Great Britain by Bookcraft, Avon

Contents

Preface

This short essay owes its origins to personal teaching experience. To be more accurate, it stems from the observation that, even now, anyone engaged in studies related to the Fathers of the Church has not had readily available any historical outline of patristic exegesis, i.e. of the most characteristic element of Christian learning in the earliest centuries. This need has not been met by the over-brief accounts to be found in relevant entries in various dictionaries and encyclopaedias. On the other hand, the more ample articles, such as that contained in the first volume of *The Cambridge History of the Bible*, limit their attention to a few outstanding figures, neglecting the connections between them and so neglecting also the line of development of exegesis. Even the recent publication of B. de Margerie (*Introduction à L'histoire de l'exégèse. I. Les Perès grecs et orientaux*, Paris 1980) does not seem to take sufficient account of this requirement.

The few pages offered here cannot expect to fill so great a gap. Their scope, rather, is merely to offer an initial, elementary aid to those embarking on the study of patristic exegesis. While it can scarcely be feasible, within such limited confines, to enter into details about authors and their works, it is however, hoped to illustrate 'high points' and significant interconnections, to trace the progressive development, the juxtapositions, and oppositions between movements and schools of thought, thus presenting an overview of the subject matter, which, however vast, is also organic and complete in itself.

Abbreviations

CCG   Corpus Christianorum, series Graeca

CCL   Corpus Christianorum, series Latina

CSCO   Corpus Scriptorum Christianorum Orientalium

CSEL   Corpus Scriptorum Ecclesiasticorum Latinorum

GCS   Die griechischen Christlichen Schriftsteller

PG   J. P. Migne, *Patrologia Graeca*

PL   J. P. Migne, *Patrologia Latina*

PLS   *Patrologia Latina, Supplementum*

PO   *Patrologia Orientalis*

SC   *Sources Chrétiennes*

Chapter 1

Scripture in the Church of the 1st and 2nd Centuries

Christianity, like Judaism, is a religion of the Book. In it, Holy Scripture, regarded as the fruit of divine revelation for the good of the Church, occupies an absolutely fundamental place: every action in the life of the community, collective or individual, from doctrine to discipline and worship, should be shaped by it. At the same time, Scripture is a complex of writings diverse in subject matter, form, and date, and sometimes inaccessible for various reasons, so that the effective knowledge and use of them by Christians was not obvious, but required a notably complex effort of interpretation. This work could be explicit and direct, dealing specifically in various literary genres (homily or commentary), with the interpretation of sacred texts ranging from a single passage to several passages or an entire book; or it could be implicit and indirect, in that the application of Scripture to the various circumstances of the community's life required the value and significance of a given text to be penetrated, so as to adapt it to needs and purposes with which it may not have had an immediate or obvious link. We might say that the whole life of the community was conditioned by the interpretation of Scripture. It has been said that the history of doctrine is the history of exegesis, in that the whole development of catholic doctrine is based on the interpretation of a certain number of passages in Scripture in the light of particular needs; but the same could be said of any other aspect of the Church's life: organisation, discipline,

1

worship, and so on. For this reason, the study of Holy Scripture was the real foundation of Christian culture in the Church of the earliest centuries. It is the methods and forms in which this study expressed itself that we shall trace here in brief historical outline. We shall glance firstly at the hermeneutical techniques in use in Jewish and Greek circles, since these exercised a strong influence on the exegetical method of Christian scholars.

1. *The Jews and the Greeks: Literalism/Allegory*

With regard to the Old Testament, the Jews were presented with the same problem as that outlined above for the Church, i.e. that of adapting the facts of the sacred text to the actual needs of the people, and of making it accessible to them at a practical level. The interpretation of the Old Testament was of central importance for Judaism from the time when, with Ezra's reform after the return of the Jews from the Babylonian captivity (6th century BC), the Old Testament, and the books of the Mosaic Law in particular, became normative for the life of the people.

There were two fundamental directions which interpretation could take. The first was of a legislative nature, aimed particularly at responding to questions arising from the practical application of the sacred text to everyday life (*halakhah*).[1] This study was practised especially in the rabbinical schools. The second (*haggadah*) had a more varied scope. It particularly concerned the edification of the faithful and had its most important application in the homily, which formed part of the worship of the synagogue.

The rabbinical method of approaching the sacred text was very meticulous, at times excessively so. It monitored the accuracy of the biblical text in question; it would explain grammatical characteristics, and would cover every detail. The interpretation of any given text was made according to different procedures: by linking it to one or more related passages of Scripture; or on the basis of a more comprehensive examination of the context, by employing *a fortiori* arguments, or comparisons.

The predominant interest was the literal approach and in fact Christians were indeed later to consider this method of interpreting Scripture as specifically Jewish. However, allegorical exegesis was not unknown either. Suffice it to recall the then current interpretation of the bridegroom and bride in the Song of Songs as symbols of Yahweh and Israel. Yet this was a marginal form of interpretation and it was only minimally developed.

The earliest Old Testament interpretation was predominantly oral, and only began to be fixed at a later stage. We might also mention at this point the literary genres of 'targum' and 'midrash'. The former was the Aramaic translation of the Bible, necessitated by the disappearance of the vernacular Hebrew. This accompanied the reading of the sacred text in the synagogues. The translation was very free, indeed properly a paraphrase.[2] Sometimes it was interpolated with halakhic or haggadic insertions. 'Midrash', on the other hand, can indicate either a particular type of 'actualising' interpretation of the Old Testament, by a process of combining different passages, or the product of the interpretation itself, i.e. the actual commentary. The Midrashim which have come down to us are of a relatively late date (4th or 5th century AD), but they make use of material which is much older. Such material has been gathered together, quoting for each verse (of Genesis or Exodus, etc.) the interpretations of different rabbis, each mentioned by name. Obviously, this collection of material has been made selectively, but the material chosen was quoted in its original form, or nearly so, without any attempt to standardise either style or content.

The discovery of the Dead Sea manuscripts has brought to our attention yet another type of Scripture commentary, which has been termed *pesher* (=explanation). Entire Old Testament books, or parts thereof, are quoted verse by verse, followed by a brief interpretation. This type of interpretation 'actualises' the biblical text (usually prophetic),[3] by relating it to the historical developments taking place in the Qumran sect, and in Palestine in general. Fragment 3 of the 'pesher' of Nahum mentions the Seleucid king Demetrius, a contemporary of the Hasmonaeans. Other figures who continually appear on the scene are the 'teacher of righteousness' and the 'wicked priest', important figures in Qumran literature. The most common reference is to the 'Kittim', a name which refers to Macedonian and Roman invaders. Here, for example, is the commentary on Habbakuk 1:10: ('they make light of all fortresses; they heap up earth and take them'), 'The interpretation refers to the commandments of the Kittim who despise the fortresses of the people and insolently mock them.... They bring them down because of the iniquity of their inhabitants' (following Moraldi's translation). In keeping with the tenor of texts of the prophets, the interpretation frequently has an eschatological significance. Sometimes it can become allegorical in the interpretation of details, as in the Pesher of Nahum, Fragment 1: Bashan is interpreted as the Kittim; Carmel as their king, Lebanon their leaders.

* * *

The Greeks did not have texts with the same normative value as Scripture, but in their schools of Rhetoric and Philosophy there was a custom of reading and explaining literary and philosophical texts, so that advanced exegetical techniques were also brought to bear on them, and among them too there was a progression from a purely oral teaching tradition to a writing down of commentaries on the poets and philosophers. A commentary on a poetic work (Homer, Virgil, etc.) is usually concise. After the quotation of one line, there follows the explanation of any difficulties of language, interpretation, or the like, and clarification of historical, mythological, and antiquarian references.

It is obvious that in the Greek and Latin scholarly tradition, as in that of the Jewish rabbis which we have mentioned, earlier interpretations were passed on in later work. For example, Eustathius' very late (12th century) commentary on the Homeric poems relays much earlier material. But, compared to the Judaic 'midrashim', the classical commentaries, as well as being more concise, are better ordered, are selective with regard to material, and usually present such material without referring by name to this or that earlier grammarian.

Commentaries on philosophical works are markedly different from those on literary works: they are much fuller, and the various authors, in their presentation of the thought of Plato, Aristotle and others, at times give interpretations which are so individual (even if on the same lines as the ancient text) as to become works of totally original speculation. We might recall Proclus' commentaries on Plato's *Dialogues*.

Alongside the literal interpretation of Homer and other poets used in scholarly circles, there was also another decidedly allegorical kind which went much further back in time. At this point, however, it should be stressed that by 'allegory' and 'to allegorise' (Greek: *allegoria/allegorein*[4] = to say other things, i.e., to say one thing in order to signify another) two quite different procedures can be implied. The first, composite, is that by which a writer expresses concepts which conceal behind the literal meaning a more significant, hidden meaning, so that the wood in which Dante loses himself at the beginning of the *Divine Comedy* is intended by the poet himself as a symbol of sin, and the three beasts he encounters there are symbols of three particular sins. The second, hermeneutical approach consists in discovering in a poetic (or other) text another meaning apart from the literal sense, and also beyond the original intentions of the author: as, for example, with Plotinus, who perceives in the hard-fought return home of Ulysses an allegory of the soul returning to its homeland. The allegory with which we are concerned here is almost exclusively of this second kind.

To understand the popularity achieved by this hermeneutical procedure in the interpretation of Homer and the Greek myths, we need to appreciate the great prestige which Homer's works enjoyed throughout the entire Greek world, to the extent that the poet even came to be regarded as of divine origin. However, philosophical reflection soon highlighted the improbability and even absurdity of these myths about gods and heroes which Homer narrated, so that, to safeguard the authority and prestige of his poems, it was supposed that he told so many obviously absurd stories about the gods with the intention of alluding to other subjects. Already in the 6th century BC, Theagenes of Rhegium understood the discord among Homer's gods as an allegory of the discord of the natural elements: heat opposed to cold, dry to wet, and so on. In the next century, Anaxagoras initiated a psychological interpretation of the Homeric gods: Zeus became the symbol of intelligence, Athene of technical ability, and so on. It was above all the Stoics who propagated this type of interpretation of the traditional deities and of the works of their bard. They did this in order to eliminate anything unsuitable which tradition attributed to the gods, and also to harmonise traditional polytheism with their own philosophical montheism by interpreting the gods as symbols of natural or other forces. At the beginning of the common era, this type of interpretation and its related terminology was widely used in scholarly circles and among people of literary and philosophical attainment.

* * *

This hermeneutical procedure and the terminology connected with it were embraced by the Hellenising strain of Judaism, especially in Alexandria, as a fundamental means of bringing about the much sought after rapprochement between the religious beliefs of the Jews which centred on the Old Testament and the Greek culture which surrounded it.

Our information in this area comes chiefly from Philo, but not exclusively (cf. also Ps.-Aristeas, Flavius Josephus, etc.). Philo himself does not conceal his use of earlier sources, showing the widespread use of this procedure.

His works are of two kinds. For the most part, they consist of commentaries on large sections of Genesis and Exodus, with references to other books of the Law, in which the biblical text is presented and commented upon with a very full interpretation recalling the Greek philosophical style of commentary. Alongside these works there are the *Quaestiones in Genesim* and *in Exodum*, which again following a method typical for the interpretation of pagan texts, set out collections of particularly significant verses from the two books together with a section-by-section commentary restricted to essentials. Both types of commentary became popular in Christian Alexandria.

The encounter between Scripture and Greek tradition culminated in making comparisons between the biblical text and Greek myths. Philo disapproved of this procedure and preferred the allegorical interpretation of the sacred text according to the norms which governed the interpretation of the Homeric poems. This method allowed him, on the one hand, to give satisfactory explanations of so many anthropomorphisms in the earlier books of the Old Testament, which, like the Greek myths, upset the sensibilities of educated pagans. On the other hand, by a process of interpretation which made plentiful use of philosophical concepts and terminology, especially Platonic and Stoic, he was able to introduce to the Greek mind a religious perceptive which had been quite foreign to it.

For Philo, the Bible has far greater importance than this or that myth might have for a pagan, so that he does not entirely ignore the literal meaning of the passage before him. But the value he assigns to it is quite secondary; it is for the many, while the hidden meaning, attainable by the allegorical approach, is for the few who concern themselves with the realities of the Spirit (*Abr.* 147). The progression from the literal to the allegorical level is facilitated by certain indicators in the text which hold special significance for the shrewd exegete. This could involve details to which (for various reasons) the literal meaning is not pertinent: names of animals or particular items, above all proper names of people or places. These are then interpreted etymologically, following a procedure given general application by the Stoics in their interpretations of the Greek gods. These are all procedures which we shall have to recall when dealing with Christian exegesis in Alexandria.

The contents of Philo's allegorical interpretation are primarily cosmological or anthropological. Suffice it to give a few examples: the Temple in Jerusalem symbolises the world; the parts of the Temple the different parts of the world (*Spec. Leg.* I, 66); the four colours of the vesture of the Jewish High Priest represent the four elements of nature (*Vit. Mos.* I, 88). In the account of the creation of man, Adam symbolises intelligence, the animals, the passions, and Eve sensitivity (*Leg. All.* II 8-9, 24, 35-38); the union of Abraham and Sarah indicates the union of intelligence and virtue (*Abr.* 99).

2. *The Old Testament in the Writers of the Apostolic and Sub-Apostolic Age*
The first Christians were Jewish both by birth and by upbringing, so they had no doubts or hesitations in accepting the Old Testament as the revelation of God to Israel, whose elect they considered themselves to be. They interpreted the Old Testament according to methods usual in Judaism of the period, in order to adapt it to their own needs. In doing this they did not limit themselves to merely embellishing their discourse with quotations from the Old Testament, either the actual text, or merely its gist, or even various combinations of the two; but they also adopted more complex procedures of the 'midrash' style in the sense that they presented new ideas, expressive of the new realities of nascent Christianity, by combining Old Testament passages reminiscent of one other: thus the 'Magnificat' (Lk. 1:46-55) represents an intertwining of Old Testament quotations and allusions combined to express a new reality.

Sometimes the procedure is more complex. In Rom. 9:6-29, Paul presents the distinction between Israel according to the spirit and Israel according to the flesh, and the mystery of divine election, in the form of a *midrash* on Gen. 21:12: 'for through Isaac shall your descendants (*sperma*) be named'; depending on Gen. 18:10: 'I will surely return to you in the spring, and Sarah your wife shall have a son', and then a series of passages connected with the inscrutable will through which God puts his call into action (Gen. 25:23; Mal. 1:2-3; Ex. 33:19, etc.). The passage which closes the *midrash*, Is. 1:9, recalls the initial text through the key word 'children' (*sperma*).

Elsewhere the procedure is developed as a question. In Matt. 15:1-9 the Pharisees put a question to Jesus about respect for the traditions; the reply of Jesus is based on Ex. 20:21 and 21:17, which deal with the respect owed by all to their father and mother, and he concludes his reasoning with Is. 29:13: 'This people... honour me with their lips, while their hearts are far from me.'

Even the *pesher* method of 'actualising' the Old Testament called is represented in the books of the New Testament. Jesus himself uses it (Lk. 4:16-21) when he reads Is. 61:1-2 in the synagogue of Nazareth: 'the Spirit of the Lord is upon me', and applies it to himself: 'this text is being fulfilled today even as you listen'. John uses the same technique when he models the beast of Rev. 13 on the four beasts of Dan. 7, but he updates the meaning by substituting the Roman Empire for the empires of earlier times.

With these examples, we can pass from the formal aspects of early Christian interpretation of the Old Testament to the actual content of that interpretation. Here the early Church's link with the Jewish tradition of the Old Testament comes into tension with the newness of the message which the Old Testament itself is used to confirm. The first Christians recognised in Jesus the Messiah foretold by the prophets and so they applied to Jesus the many Old Testament passages which were commonly understood at the time to be messianic. But the majority of the Jews did not accept this message, and the resulting debates became centred on these prophecies and their applicability to events in the life of Christ. The writings of the New Testament show widespread signs of these discussions centred on the interpretation of the messianic passages in the Old Testament: Matt. 22:41-46 and 21:42-43 present Christ as applying to himself Pss. 109:1 and 117:22-23; and the speeches of Peter in the early chapters of Acts are interwoven with messianic texts applied to Christ.

The messianic character of many passages in the Old Testament was recognised by both Christians and Jews, even if the latter did not accept their applicability to Christ. But the novelty of Christ, as a suffering and crucified Messiah, where the Jews were expecting a Messiah who would triumph over Israel's enemies, led Christians to interpret in a prophetic and christological sense Old Testament passages other than those usually understood as messianic, such as Ps. 117:22-23: 'The stone which the builders rejected has become the head of the corner'; and, above all, sections of Deutero-Isaiah on the Suffering Servant of Yahweh. It will suffice to recall, in this connection, the encounter between Philip and the Ethiopian in Acts 8: 26ff. with its quotation and interpretation of Is. 53:7-8.[5]

We can locate the first Christian anthologies or *Testimonia* within this polemical context. The Dead Sea manuscripts have shown us that the Jews had already been accustomed to making anthologies of Old Testament excerpts. The Christians quickly adopted this method to gather together passages which helped to underline the distinctive character of their creed, as opposed to the common faith of the Jews: messianic texts, passages on the interpretation of the Law, and so on. Extant anthologies of this type, e.g. Cyprian's *Testimonia ad Quirinum*, are very late, but the recurrence of the same passages, sometimes in identical combinations, in the books of the New Testament proves that such collections had been in use for some time in the early Church.

On the other hand, the need for a deeper understanding of the significance of Christ and his ministry in relation to Jewish tradition induced some Christians to take an interest in the Old Testament which went far beyond the parameters set by these collections of passages. In Stephen's speech (Acts 7: 2ff.) the presentation of the Christ-event is located within a reconsideration of the whole history of Israel, seen in terms of a continuous prevarication by a people habitually inattentive to the will of God. Paul, at Antioch in Pisidia (Acts 13:17ff) inserts the same message in a historical framework which sees Christ as the pinnacle of the whole of Israel's history.

In another direction, christological reflection came to be convinced that the figure of Christ could not be understood simply as a human being, even one specially privileged by God, but rather required that he should have a genuinely divine dimension. To support this conviction, recourse was had once more to the Old Testament; Hebrews 1 presents a selection of texts which aims to present Christ as a being higher than the angels: (Ps. 2:7; Deut. 32:43; Ps. 104:4; etc.). And when John, at the beginning of the Fourth Gospel, presents Christ as the Logos of God and God himself, he develops the concept by attributing to him the distinctive characteristics of 'Wisdom' in the Old Testament.

But if there was a general conviction among all Christians that Christ was the Messiah and that the Old Testament messianic prophecies were fulfilled in him, those who were of a more rigidly Jewish persuasion were not prepared to recognise an authentically divine nature in Christ. In these conservative circles, faith in Christ became enmeshed in a religious and cultural network of particularly strict Jewish observance in which the old Law retained all its vigour; Matt. 5:17ff. has Jesus solemnly endorsing its full and permanent validity. This has all the signs of being a polemical position *vis à vis* other Christians who felt themselves less constrained by their Jewish heritage and by the literal observance of its norms; and who felt greater allegiance to the deeper spirit of the message of Christ. This tendency was represented, after Stephen, primarily by Paul.

Paul, reflecting on Scripture in the light of Christ, sees a hidden mystery (Rom. 16:25; 1 Cor. 2:1; etc.) which only the life-giving spirit can reveal, not the letter which kills (2 Cor. 3: 6). Read in this perspective, the old Law takes on a new dimension: true circumcision is that of the heart, for the one who is a Jew not just by appearance, but inwardly (Rom. 2:28f.; cf. Acts 7:51). The Law was written for us, Paul says in connection with Deut. 25:4: 'You shall not muzzle an ox when it treads out the grain', which he understands to mean that the one who works should have the hope of sharing the fruits of his work (1 Cor. 9:9). Nor does this Pauline procedure of adapting the Law in the light of a spiritual rather than literal reading stop at legal precepts. For the Jews the all-embracing term 'the Law' covered all five books of Moses, including the narrative sections; and here, too, Paul sees the mystery of Christ, in that these ancient events prefigured the events of Christ and the Church, and only these new events can provide the key for understanding the deeper meaning of the ancient ones.

Seen in this new light, Adam is presented as a prefiguration (*typos*) of Christ,[6] the Israelites, crossing the Red Sea a symbol of baptism; the Manna and the water miraculously springing from the rock in Ex. 17:6 are prefigurations of the eucharist (1 Cor. 10:1ff.). In the Fourth Gospel, the bronze serpent of Num. 21:9 and the paschal lamb of Ex. 12:1ff. prefigure the crucifixion and death of Christ (Jn. 3:14; 19:36). In Heb. 7:1, Melchizedek is a figure of Christ and in 9:9 the Temple sacrifice prefigures the sacrifice of Christ. In Heb. 10:1 the Law is said in a general way to contain the shadow of future realities, namely Christ and the Church.

As can be clearly seen, the hermeneutical procedure which Paul and the other New Testament authors use to interpret the

Law in a spiritual sense is allegorical, in that a meaning other
than the literal or immediate sense is perceived from the given
text. The usual term which Paul employs to define the
relationship between the two levels of meaning is *typos* = form,
figure, symbol or prefiguration (Rom. 5:14; I Cor. 10:6; etc.);
but in Gal. 4:24, where he presents the sons of Hagar and Sarah
as prefigurations of the Jews and Christians, he says 'Now this
is an allegory' (*allégoroumena*), showing that he regarded 'typos'
as synonymous with 'allegory'. In deference to Paul's
terminology, modern scholars call this kind of interpretation
– which, as we shall see, enjoyed immense success and became
the authentic Christian way of reading the Old Testament –
'typology' or 'typological interpretation'. In antiquity it was
called 'spiritual' or 'mystical'.[7] It was rooted in the firm
conviction that the old Law was consistently directed towards
the great Christ-event, and that, as a result, it would give up its
true significance only to those who interpreted it in
christological terms.

* * *

The sparse literature surviving from the sub-apostolic period
(the end of the 1st and the beginning of the 2nd centuries)
continued to display the same diverse attitudes towards the
Old Testament as we have seen in the New Testament. Clement's
Letter to the Corinthians, despite the obvious Hellenistic cultural
influences which have merged with the Judaeo-Christian
element, makes extensive use of the Old Testament in its literal
sense only: the great final prayer (59-61) is a weaving together
of Old Testament references taken from the most diverse
books: the Law, the historical books, the prophets, Wisdom
literature, and the great figures of the Old Testament are
repeatedly brought in as *exempla* to support Clement's
exhortation to harmony and peace. The fateful effects of
jealousy are illustrated from Cain, Esau, Aaron, and so on (4).
Examples of obedience are found in Enoch, Noah, Abraham,
Lot and Rahab (9-12); the merits of humility are displayed in
the example of Abraham, Job and David (17-18); and so we
could continue. We might notice, from our present point of

view, that some of these figures, and others which are occasionally mentioned (Joseph, Moses), are given christological touches, something otherwise absent apart from a marginal reference to the scarlet cord of Rahab (Josh. 2:18) as a *typos* of the blood of Christ (12:7). Indeed, this very allusion shows that Clement was familiar with the Pauline style of christological interpretation of the Old Testament, which was becoming established at this time, and the fact that he presents only one passing instance of it might show a reserved attitude towards this type of interpretation. In fact, in Judaeo-Christian circles more radical than that represented here by Clement, there was an explicit condemnation of any non-literal interpretation of Scripture: (Ps.-Clem., *Recog.* X 42).[8]

This kind of interpretation is represented in this period by the letter of Ps.-Barnabas. However, before examining it, we might mention another instance of silence which can hardly be regarded as accidental. I refer to the letters of Ignatius in which references to the Old Testament are very infrequent – not more than five or six altogether, with total exclusion of the books of the Law. This attitude indicates a certain suspicion, not to say aversion of some Christian circles of pagan origin, *vis-à-vis* the Old Testament, reflecting a strongly anti-Jewish approach. The radicalisation of this attitude will be seen in Gnosticism.

At the opposite extreme to Ignatius' position, Ps.-Barnabas is profoundly interested in the Old Testament. His Judaeo-Christian origins can be seen, apart from other indications, in the midrashic procedures which he uses to interpret Scripture; but his Jewish-Christian outlook is close to that of Paul and Hebrews and shows itself, in relation to the Old Testament, in his radicalisation of Paul's position. Paul had never disputed that the Law had a real value for the Jews; however, Ps.-Barnabas interprets the episode of Ex. 32:15ff. in which Moses smashes the tablets of the law, as a sign that the Jews because of their unworthiness did not deserve the Covenant which God wished to make with them, and that this had instead been transferred to the Christians (4:6-8; 14:1-5). Consequently, he maintains that the Jews were wrong to have applied the precepts of the Law literally instead of understanding them spiritually.

Thus, with typically midrashic method, he interprets allegorically, for example, the dietary regulations: to refrain from eating pig's flesh signifies having no contact with men who behave like pigs; to abstain from eating the hare signifies avoiding pederasty, and so on (10). In 9:8, in the symbolic interpretation of the circumcision of Abraham, he interprets the number 318, the number of Abraham's servants, as symbolic of the name of Jesus and of the cross, following a procedure for the symbolic interpretation of numbers used by the Jews themselves, but particularly widespread among the Greeks and Hellenised Jews. In this sense, the seven days of creation are interpreted as a symbol of the six thousand years' duration of the world and of the last judgment by Christ (= the Sabbath): (15). Typological interpretation, too[9], is extended by Ps.-Barnabas, in comparison with Pauline usage, with greater attention to details: the sacrifice of Jesus is prefigured by the ceremonies of the day of fasting, by the scapegoat, and by the sacrifice of the heifer (7-8); the prayer said by Moses with hands extended during the battle between the Israelites and the Amalekites is seen as a 'typos' of the cross and the crucified (12:2-3); Joshua is a figure of Christ (12:8-10).

We might think to locate in such Christian circles, and more or less in this period, the origin of certain symbols which come to enjoy great success: the sun as a symbol of Christ, the moon and the boat as symbols of the Church, the sea as a symbol of the world.[10]

3. *Gnostic Interpretation of Scripture*

While Clement's manner of interpretation was aimed at fostering the acceptance by the Church of the Old Testament, now relieved of many typically Jewish prescriptions as a normative code for morality alongside the New Testament, the interpretative style of Ps.-Barnabas became ever more established as the specifically Christian method of reading the Old Testament. Radical reinterpretation in a typological vein secured the authority of the Old Testament for the Church which was now under attack from the Gnostics. Their dualism and their disregard for the material world led them also to disdain the Old Testament as being the revelation of the God of creation, the Demiurge, in contrast to the New Testament, the revelation of the supreme, good God. Yet, at the same time, it was precisely from the Old Testament that they derived certain fundamental features of their origins and nature. The combination of these two attitudes led to an interpretation of the Old Testament which, on the one hand, tended to place the Demiurge in a poor light through literal interpretation of the anthropomorphisms which are so plentiful in the earlier books of Scripture;[11] and which, on the other, interpreted a few important episodes in such a way as to reconcile them with certain strongholds of Gnostic doctrine and tradition. As a typical example of this we could cite a page of the *Gospel of Truth* (NHC IX 3:45ff.) in which the Gnostic author gives a positive presentation of Adam and Eve's transgression of the prohibition against eating from the tree of good and evil, a transgression inspired by the serpent, the wisest of all the animals, so that the couple might acquire knowledge of their real nature, and then asks himself, against the background of the material narrated in Gen. 1-3, what kind of god this is, who shows himself to be jealous, ignorant and malicious?

In various Gnostic texts these events are interpreted in a pointedly mythical way, to show how Sophia (= the Divine Logos) has infused the seed of a spiritual nature into the 'psychic' or 'material' man created by the archons through the will of the Demiurge. This rendered man superior to the Demiurge, with the result that the latter tries to recover or else neutralise this somehow.[12]

The positive evaluation of the sin of Adam sometimes extends into a form of interpretation, hostile to the Demiurge, which exalts figures presented in a negative light by the Old Testament: Cain, the people of Sodom, Esau, and so on. For this reason one Gnostic sect adopted the name 'Cainites' after Cain, the first man to oppose the Demiurge, the prototype of the 'spiritual' man, i.e. the Gnostic. A text of Hippolytus (*Ref.* V 16:4-13) dealing with the Perates, connects together a series of people and events in the Old Testament to constitute a complete 'sacred history' in opposition to the Demiurge, in which the serpent is taken as symbol of the Logos : Eve, Cain, Joseph, Esau, Jacob, Nimrod, the Bronze Serpent,[13] and so on, concluding with a quotation of the Prologue of John.

While some Gnostics entirely rejected the Old Testament on the grounds that 'all the prophets and the Law spoke through the power of the Demiurge, a foolish god; they also were foolish and knew nothing' (Hippolytus, *Ref.* VI 35:1), others took up a more complex and nuanced position. In the *Letter to Flora*, Ptolemy, the Valentinian (mid 2nd century), took an intermediate stance towards the Law, somewhere between the total acceptance of the catholics and the radical rejection of the Marcionites. He makes a threefold distinction: unjust legislation, destined to be abolished by the Saviour; imperfect legislation, destined to be perfected; and legislation which had a merely symbolic value. Underpinning this evaluation is the conviction that Sophia also had contributed to the Old Testament, through the Demiurge, even if only spasmodically, and unknown to him, so that while some prophecies derive from the Demiurge, others are from Sophia herself (Irenaeus, *Adv. Haer.* I 7:3, I 30:11).

In the same way of thinking, the *Apocryphon of John* on several occasions reproves Moses for not speaking accurately about the Spirit which hovered over the waters, about the sin of Eve, about the sleep of Adam, about Noah's ark (BG 45, 58, 59, 61, 73): we should understand the reproof in the sense that Moses, inspired not only by the Demiurge but also by Sophia, wrote things which in their spiritual sense transcended his capacities as a mere 'psychic' man, and so dealt with them in a manner not corresponding to the reality of the facts. So, for certain privileged texts of the Old Testament, these Gnostics distinguish two sources of inspiration: the Demiurge, who inspires the literal, psychical meaning of the text intended for 'psychic' men, and Sophia, who inspires a deeper meaning, the spiritual one intended for Gnostics only.

In point of fact, the Gnostics were masterly in allegorical exegesis and made use of it in various contexts, quite apart from the highly technical ones which we have examined. Suffice it to recall the so-called preaching of the Naassenes (Hippolytus, *Ref.* V 7:2ff.), in which passages from the Old Testament and New Testament are used together with Greek poetry and various myths to symbolise the divine element which was degraded and imprisoned in the world of which it is the vital principle. It is symbolised by the cup which Joseph hides in Benjamin's sack of grain, symbol of the body (V 8:6 on Gen. 44:1ff.). And in the *Great Revelation* of the Simonians on the basis of Is. 44:2, 24: 'I who made you, who formed you in the womb', Paradise, in which Adam was formed, is taken as a symbol of the mother's womb in which God forms every man: Paradise is the womb; Eden the placenta; the river which flows from Eden, the umbilical cord, and so on (Hippolytus, *Ref.* VI 14:7-8).

* * *

The time has now come to discuss the interpretation of the New Testament. The writings gathered together as the New Testament re-echoed in various ways by the sub-apostolic authors but not yet canonised by a *corpus* parallel to the Old Testament, were adopted by the Gnostics, or rather by certain more christianised Gnostics, as works which were fully authoritative, in contrast to the Old Testament, since they were the Revelation of Christ himself, the Son of the supreme God. We could recall, in this connection, that the first canon of the New Testament was that laid down by Marcion based on the Pauline tradition (the letters and the Third Gospel).

While the Old Testament was readily interpreted by the Gnostics in a literal manner, we have seen why, for the New Testament, they used a markedly allegorical exegesis to square the scriptural data with the various facets of their own doctrine. Our information about this interpretative method comes mainly from the Valentinians, the most christianised and also the most sophisticated of all the Gnostics. To judge by the evidence of Irenaeus, they used number symbolism extensively but superficially e.g. the 1st, 3rd, 6th, 9th and 11th hours in the parable of Matt. 20:1ff. (the workers in the vineyard) symbolise the thirty aeons of the Pleroma, since the sum of these numbers is thirty (Irenaeus, *Adv. Haer.* I 1:3). We also know that Marcus Magus extended this type of interpretation so as to reduce all Gnostic doctrine to numerical relationships. Yet, elsewhere Gnostic interpretation even in its arbitrariness, was very subtle: the three types of human nature (material, psychic and spiritual) are indicated respectively by Matt. 8:19f., in which Jesus replies to those wishing to follow him, 'the Son of Man has nowhere to lay his head'; by Lk. 9:61f., in which Jesus replies to the man who wishes to follow him but first wished to make his farewells to his people, 'no-one who puts his hand to the plough and looks back is fit for the kingdom of God'; by Matt. 8:22, in which Jesus says to the man who wanted to bury his father first: 'Leave the dead to bury their dead.' In fact the first response is understood as a refusal, the second as a warning, and the third as a command, and thus they characterise the wicked nature of material men, the intermediate state of the psychics and the good nature of the spiritual men (Irenaeus, *Adv. Haer.* I 8:3).

The Valentinians valued the Fourth Gospel especially, for it lent itself well to a Gnostic interpretation. We have a long passage in which Ptolemy interprets John's Prologue, doctrinally the most pregnant section, with a subtle play of references to derive the names of the Ogdoad, the most important members of the Pleroma: Father, Grace, Son, Truth, Logos, Life, Man, Church (Irenaeus, *Adv. Haer.* I 8:5-6). We ought not to consider it accidental that Heraclaeon made a systematic commentary on this Gospel – the first specifically exegetical Christian text of which we have certain knowledge. From the forty-nine fragments which still survive we can conclude that the commentary did not extend to the end of the Gospel, and did not systematically examine every single verse, although it was fairly comprehensive and not merely a collection of certain selected passages (scholia). The commentary which followed line by line after the text of John's Gospel, seems to have been fairly concise, in the style of Greek literary commentaries.

While Ptolemy's commentary on John's Prologue highlights technical Gnostic doctrine, and was intended for use within the community, Heraclaeon's commentary was devised for a wider and more diverse readership and it purposely avoids touching on arguments which are too technical, and settles on the two fundamental points of doctrine: the distinction between the supreme God of the New Testament and the Demiurge of the Old Testament; and the distinguishing of people into three different natures by origin and by destiny.

To give just a small example, the Demiurge and the whole 'psychic substance' are symbolised by the court official whose son was ill in Jn. 4:46 (Frag. 40), the spiritual man is symbolised by the Samaritan woman (Frag. 17ff.) the material man is symbolised by the Jews to whom Jesus says (Jn. 8:44), 'your father [is] the devil' (Frag. 44-47). The interpretation of the Baptist is especially subtle – on the boundary between the old and new dispensations, he acts sometimes as a psychic man, other times, as a spiritual man (Frag. 3ff.).

Heraclaeon's interpretation is predominately allegorical, but does not totally disregard the literal sense of the text (Frag. 32, 39, etc.); some passages are interpreted first literally and then allegorically (Frag. 8, 22); the relationship between the two types of interpretation is a flexible one and cannot be reduced to a simple rule.

His allegory is based upon the symbolic value of numbers, supposed difficulties in the literal reading of the text (as in Philo), and it can exploit the smallest details of the text. For example, in Jn. 1:23: 'I am the voice of one crying in the wilderness, etc,' the inferiority of John compared to Christ, i.e. of the psychic compared to the spiritual man, is derived from the feminine gender of the word *phone* (= voice) compared with the masculine of *logos* (word), referring to Christ (Frag. 5). Capernaum is taken to be a symbol of matter because it is situated on the bank of the lake = stagnant water – a symbol of the world (Frag. 11, 40). Heraclaeon could clearly apply the exegetical method of pagan and Philonic allegory with some finesse.

4. *Anti-Jewish and Anti-Gnostic Controversies*
Christianity of the second century had become strongly Hellenised; it had, however, inherited controversies with regard to the Old Testament, following its acceptance and christological interpretation of it. It had to defend this position in the second part of the century on two separate fronts: against Judaism and against Gnosticism. Justin and Irenaeus show us the two approaches, which fundamentally overlap, in spite of their different objectives.

Justin takes a less radical stand on the Law than Ps.-Barnabas, in the sense that he can distinguish between the prescriptions of natural morality and legal prescriptions: the former are valid permanently, but the latter are now devoid of value. He does not deny that the Law had its value in its day, even if it was given to the Jews because of their inability to observe a spiritual law.

But for him, as for Paul and Ps.-Barnabas, the Law is above all a *typos* of the future reality of Christ and the Church. He articulates the concept in an anti-Jewish manner, distinguishing between *typoi* and *logoi* (= prophecies): 'Sometimes the Holy Spirit clearly enacted what was a *typos* of future events; at other times, he pronounced prophecies (*logous*) relating to events which would come about' (*Dial.* 114:1). Only the incarnation of Christ has unveiled the real meaning of the Old Testament for us (*Dial.* 100:2) The Jews were mistaken in that they interpreted the *typoi* at face value (112) and because they did not wish to recognise that the prophecies were fulfilled in Christ.

In applying this hermeneutical criterion, Justin, as also Irenaeus and the other writers of the Asian school, refers *typoi* and *logoi* to concrete events in the life of Christ and of the Church; he does not recognise the spiritual application, which was to be the particular domain of the Alexandrians. Nor does he apply it systematically, as Origen was to do. Instead, he concentrates on a few events and institutions, while further broadening the typological perspective of Ps.-Barnabas. It will be sufficient to recall, for example, the correlation of Eve and Mary as antitypes (*Dial.* 100:4-5); the twofold eschatological (*2 Apol.* 7) and christological/baptismal interpretation of the Flood (*Dial.* 138); the highlighting of the Joshua/Jesus typology outside the books of the Law (*Dial.* 113).[14]

Justin also extended the argument from prophecy, e.g. he is thus the first to our knowledge to connect Is. 33:16 with the cave at Bethlehem (*Dial.* 78:6).[15] To develop this theme, Justin makes frequent use of *testimonia* and sometimes without realising uses scripture passages which had been adapted and modified by a 'targum' procedure, to underline their christological significance. Consequently, he accuses the Jews of having altered these texts: for example, of having eliminated from Ps. 95:10 the expression 'from the wood' which, in fact, was an addition made by the Christians in order to connect the reign of Christ with the cross (*Dial.* 73). Limited linguistic skills constituted a particular limitation of the exegesis of Justin and of the other authors of Asiatic training.

In his dispute with the Gnostics Irenaeus develops the same typological interpretation of the Old Testament, but with a different purpose: his intention is to show that there is really no break between the old and the new dispensations, since as both are directed by the providence of the one God, who first of all used the Law to teach, then the prophets to train gradually human beings to enter into communion with him and to be able, through the Incarnation of Christ, to pass *per typica ad vera et per temporalia ad aeterna et per carnalia ad spiritualia et per terrena ad caelestia* (*Adv. Haer.* IV 14:2-3; IV 9:3; IV 20:5, 8). Christ was hidden like the treasure in the field (Matt. 13:44) and only his coming had allowed us to discover this (*Adv. Haer.* IV 26:1), after the prophets (i.e. for Irenaeus, the whole Old Testament) had foretold him by word, by vision and by symbolic action (*Adv. Haer.* IV 20:8).

Irenaeus' use of typology is thoroughly traditional and, at times, he explicitly appeals to the authority of the Elders (Lot as a figure of Christ: IV 31). He repeats Justin's distinction between *typoi* and prophecies (IV 20:8), but expands his procedure, developing eschatological interpretation in particular (the calamities afflicting the Egyptians become a *typos* of those in the Book of Revelation which will afflict all peoples: IV 30:4). Above all we see his expansion of the procedure in his interpretation of details: e.g. in the dietary prescription of Lev. 11:2ff.; to eat animals that part the hoof and chew the cud is taken as referring to Christians, pagans and Jews; the first are symbolised by animals which are clean, in that they chew the cud, i.e. meditate on the Law of God day and night, and part the hoof, i.e. have a stable faith in the Father and the Son; pagans are symbolised by animals which neither chew the cud nor part the hoof, because they lack both the characteristics of Christians; the Jews, finally, are represented by animals which chew the cud but which do not part the hoof, because they meditate on the Law of God, but do not believe in Christ (V 8:3).[16] In Irenaeus there also appears a practice already touched upon when we considered Philo, in which typological allegory is based on a supposed deficiency in the literal sense: if we were to interpret literally the blessing given by Isaac to Jacob, we would find ourselves in great difficulty, like the Jews, because the blessings foretold by Isaac to his son have not been realised. This indicates that the passage (Gen. 27:27ff.) is to be understood only in a figurative way, in reference to the good things which the righteous will enjoy in the millenary reign of Christ (V 33:3). Periodically, we also see in Irenaeus what one might call 'vertical' allegory, which was to achieve much popularity in the Alexandrian school, and which consists in seeing sacred earthly realities (the Temple, the tent) as the *typos* of heavenly realities: IV 19:1. With regard to the importance which Irenaeus, too, gives to the argument from prophecy, suffice it to point out that the entire second part of the *Demonstratio*, from chap. 57 onwards, is a systematic collection of the main christological prophecies, presented in order following the life of Christ, from birth to resurrection and ascension.

* * *

What information we have on Justin shows him to be interested in the Old Testament only in terms of disagreement with the Jews;[17] he has no need to tackle problems of hermeneutics. He is basically literalist in his efforts to show that prophecies were fulfilled in Christ, and allegoralist in his typological interpretation of the Law in terms of Christ. We have already seen him reprove the Jews for their mistaken literal understanding of *typoi* (*Dial.* 112).[18]

Irenaeus, on the other hand, engaged against the Gnostics, finds himself in a very different situation. He uses the allegorical method to read the Old Testament christologically, and thus to link the two Testaments, but he is perfectly aware that the Gnostics use the same interpretative method to give their teachings scriptural authority. He recognises that in the New Testament there are *multae parabolae et allegoriae*, which the Gnostics can manipulate *in ambiguum* and adapt *dolose ad figmentum suum* (*Adv. Haer.* I 3:6); he accuses them of forcing the meaning of the Scriptures (I 8:1); he denies that prophetic texts can be allegorised to refer to the end of the world (V 35:1); yet, he himself only a few pages previously had interpreted Gen. 27:27 allegorically in an eschatological vein.

Although Irenaeus expresses the sound principle of interpreting obscure texts of Scripture in the light of clearer ones (II 27:1; II 28:3), he is in fact unable to find a valid hermeneutical principle to oppose the allegorical interpretation of his adversaries, chiefly because he does not really concern himself with determining, even approximately, the relationship between allegorical and literal interpretation. I mean by this not so much that Irenaeus, like Justin, sees in Christ the fulfilment of Old Testament prophecies read literally, as that he can find significant possibilities for a literal reading even in the books of the Law, usually read as christological allegories. This is especially the case in *Dem.* 11-29, which gives an account of sacred history from Adam to Moses, in which the events recounted in Genesis and Exodus are taken in the most literal and obvious sense. Suffice it to add that in *Adv. Haer.* V 20:2 and 23:1, i.e. within the space of only a few pages, God's instruction to Adam concerning the fruit in Paradise (Gen. 2:16) is interpreted first allegorically – make use of all Scripture, but without pride, or having contact with heretics – and then literally. It is clear that Irenaeus considered it to be normal that, for certain passages of Scripture, the allegorical sense should be superimposed on the literal one, but he never felt the need to elucidate the ways in which this superimposition of meanings operated.

The same observation applies to the interpretation of the New Testament, which Irenaeus, like his adversaries, habitually uses as a *corpus* of writings which are now canonised and considered normative, and where we would expect a systematically literalist approach to counter arbitrary Gnostic allegorising. Such interpretation is indeed predominant, but it is sometimes accompanied by an allegorical reading, especially in the interpretation of the details of parables, which Irenaeus readily interprets in relation to salvation history (IV 36:1-2: the parable of the wicked husbandmen). So too the unjust judge of Lk. 18:2ff. is also seen as a figure of the antichrist, while the widow who, unmindful of God, applies to him for help is a symbol of the earthly Jerusalem (V 25:4). Just as the people of the Old Testament prefigure the Church here and now, so the present Church prefigures the Church of the end-times (IV 22:2), a sequence of ideas later exploited by Origen.[19]

It is understandable that Irenaeus, not having any clear hermeneutical principle of his own, should in his opposition to the Gnostics have attacked their interpretation of Scripture at the level of content rather than at the level of exegetical theory (II 20-25) and should therefore have felt it necessary to resort to the principle of authority: the Catholic Church alone is the touchstone of truth in the interpretation of Scripture in that it is the storehouse of authentic apostolic tradition (*Adv. Haer.* III 1-5).

As far as Tertullian is concerned, it will be enough to touch briefly on the fact that he also shared the awkward position of Irenaeus, aggravated by the fact that he had a greater number of opponents: Gnostics, Jews, and pagans. He can reject the allegorical interpretation which pagans gave to the myth of Saturn, equating him with time (*Nat.* II 12:17), while accepting the use of traditional typology against Jews and Marcionites; and in this context he can speak cheerfully of the *aenigmata, allegoriae* and *parabolae* of the Old Testament, *aliter intelligenda quam scripta sunt* (*Adv. Marc.* III 5:3), while condemning the excessive allegorism of the Gnostics in connection with, for example, the resurrection (*De Resurr.* 19:2) and appealing for a greater *simplicitas* (*De Anima* 35:2; *Adv. Prax.* 13:4). The appeal applies particularly to the books of the New Testament, for example to passages in the Gospels which teach that one should not shirk martyrdom, and which the Gnostics willingly interpreted metaphorically (*Scorp.* 11:4). And yet he sometimes admits that Christ himself made use of allegory (*allegorizavit, Adv. Marc.* IV 17:12; *De Resurr.* 37:4). It is not surprising then that Tertullian, like Irenaeus, should have resorted to the principle of authority: the authenticity and antiquity of catholic interpretation of the Scriptures (*Praescr.* 20-21 and passim).

* * *

In the authors whom we have considered, literal and allegorical interpretation of Scripture (whether of Old or New Testament) can alternate without being governed by any precise rules, following instead the needs which the author was required to meet, in situations which were polemical rather than exegetical. The general impression given by the admittedly fragmentary data at our disposal is that interest in typology was concentrated on the books of the Law, or other related books (Joshua). The content of Genesis 1-3 (creation of the world and of man, sin and punishment) represents an important exception to this tendency. Here there is a trend towards literal exegesis, parallel to the similarly literal interpretation of passages in both the Old and New Testaments relating to the end of the world (prophetic passages, especially in Isaiah, and Revelation). In these the doctrinal concern underlying the literal interpretation is evident: Justin, Irenaeus and Tertullian are millenarians and their materialist eschatology induces them to oppose the spiritualism of the Gnostics on the basis of a literal exegesis of the texts cited above.

In the literal interpretation of Gen. 1-3 we see again the aim of opposing the distorted, mythical interpretation which Gnostics gave to this text; but here we must remember that the fundamentally materialistic outlook typical of Asiatic culture led these authors not to give too much weight to the crude anthropomorphisms of the biblical narrative which so much scandalised readers of the more spiritualising tendency. It might be recalled that Theophilus of Antioch, who belonged to the same cultural environment, has left us a long treatise on salvation history from Adam through to the descendants of his sons, written by way of contrast to the ancient histories of the pagan nations (*Ad. Autol.* II 10-32). The narrative reports all the details of the biblical account, with no reservations about even the most naïve anthropomorphisms: God walking in paradise, speaking with Adam, and so on (II 22).[20] The few traces of allegory (the first three days of creation being symbolic of the Trinity, the different stars representing prophets, the righteous and sinners, etc. (III 15:16) do not have Philo's aim of eliminating absurdities of the literal sense, but are superimposed upon it, without excluding it. It appears as an occasional technique.

On the whole, the writers of Asiatic background in their interpretation of Scripture tend to be concerned with diverse and contrasting pressures: the need to read the Old Testament christologically, against Jews and Gnostics, pushed them towards allegory, while an underlying materialism and the need to oppose the exaggerated allegorism of the Gnostics encouraged a literal interpretation of the biblical text. Hence the inconsistencies we have observed in their exegesis.

5. *The Paschal Homilies: Hippolytus*

The writings of Justin, Irenaeus and Tertullian, which we have considered have been controversial and doctrinal. We move now to a quite different literary genre, to examine two paschal homilies. These too came from Asia Minor between the second half of the 2nd century and the beginning of the 3rd. One is by Melito of Sardis, the other by an unknown author, is known as *In Sanctum Pascha*.[21] They are texts which were preached to a congregation, on a liturgical feast of special solemnity. The setting has determined the rhythmical prose style, highly wrought in the Asian manner, with a close-knit interplay of short periods, connected by anaphora, alliteration, repetition, and a multitude of other rhetorical devices. Our interest in these texts is that, following Jewish practice, the Christian celebration of Easter was based on the reading and interpretation of Ex. 12, which recounts the institution of the Jewish Passover.

Both texts, following Quartodeciman observance in their special concentration on the passion of Christ, develop the fundamental typology which recognises in the Jewish Passover a figure of the Christian Pascha and perceives in the sacrifice of the lamb the passion of Christ. From this common basis, the two authors develop the relationship between the two Passovers differently. Melito concentrates his typology particularly in the first part of his text, giving a christological interpretation of the ancient rite, with references to the sin of Adam, and to the predictions of the passion contained in the Law and the prophets. In the second part, he condemns the ingratitude of Israel towards the Saviour and concludes with an exaltation of the resurrection. The other homily establishes a closer relationship between its two parts. The first presents the *typoi* – the Law in general and the Jewish Passover in particular; the second part presents the realisation of the *typoi* – the coming of Christ in general, and the passion in particular. Both authors, mistakenly linking the word *Pascha* with the Greek *paschein* (= to suffer), relate the details of the Exodus account typologically to the circumstances of Jesus' passion. In the *In Sanctum Pascha*, which makes detailed observations to this effect, the period of keeping the lamb (Ex. 12:6) prefigures the time of Jesus' imprisonment by the High Priest (chap. 12); while the sacrifice of the lamb in the evening (ibid.) designates the hour when Jesus was put to death (chap. 23), and so on.

* * *

With Hippolytus,[22] catholic exegesis, restricted so far to controversial, catechetical or doctrinal purposes, at last frees itself from these fetters and becomes an independent literary genre, with works devoted explicitly to the interpretation, if not yet of an entire book of the Bible, at least of fairly extensive passages, as the Gnostic Heraclaeon had already done with the Gospel of John. These are works in which the relevant text is quoted section by section, each section followed by an explanation which is generally concise, but not without anti-heretical observations on doctrine, and sometimes with ethical or exhortatory implications. On the whole, they resemble less the diffuse commentaries of Philo than the literary commentaries of the pagan world or the Qumran *pesharim* of Judaism.

While the treatise *On the Antichrist* (really an anthology of eschatological scripture passages, connected to form an organic whole) uses the Old Testament and New Testament equally, the commentaries proper – the *Commentary on Daniel, Commentary on the Song of Songs, David and Goliath, The Blessing of Jacob, The Blessing of Moses* – are all on the Old Testament. This may be a sign of an anti-Gnostic concern (although this does not appear to be predominant in the explanation of details), or indeed of the greater prestige which our author assigned to the ancient books in comparison with the more recent New Testament. It is perhaps symptomatic that his deep interest in eschatology led him to a systematic interpretation, not of Revelation, which was widely in evidence in the treatise *On the Antichrist*, but rather of the Book of Daniel.

Apart from the obvious link with Irenaeus, Hippolytus seems to have been influenced by earlier exegetical traditions which had in large part reached him orally. But we have to think of traditions which were limited to general exegetical themes, as well as still fluid, and which Hippolytus both fixed precisely, in selecting the material known to him, and also and especially enriched and broadened, by extending some typologies from one context to another, and by the exact interpretation of details.

While the commentaries of Hippolytus may be ideologically and doctrinally consistent, they are less so in regard to exegetical technique. Lacking a precise, relative chronology, they may be given an order which presents them in terms of an interpretative method of increasing refinement and coherence. At the start of this line of development, we can locate the *Commentary on Daniel*, in which various important episodes of this book are explained in a primarily literal way.[23] Written during a period of persecution, perhaps at the time of Septimius Severus, the commentary concretises the biblical text on the theme of martyrdom, with frequent exhortatory passages. It interprets the symbols of the statue and of the beast in an anti-Roman manner (SC 14, 144, 270ff.), and takes interest in chronological calculations of the end of the world (pp. 292ff.). Typology is concentrated almost exclusively on the Susanna episode, following its literal interpretation. Susanna is a *typos* of the Church, her husband Joachim of Christ; the two elders, of Jews and pagans respectively, enemies of the Church (p. 96). But the interpretation is barely sketched and only a few details are fitted to the basic typology. A reading of *David and Goliath* leads to the same conclusion. The typology of David as Christ is in evidence only occasionally (CSCO 264, 5,13), and the occasional allegory (the two hills are symbols of the two laws (p. 6), Jonathan is a figure of Israel (p. 20f.)) is lost in the predominately literal interpretation. Even the principal feature of the text, the contest between David and Goliath, is presented only in its literal sense.

Typological interpretation becomes more coherent in the *Commentary on the Song of Songs*: the symbolism, already traditional, of bridegroom/Christ; bride/Church (a Christian transferral of the Jewish allegory: Yahweh/Israel) is now systematically developed from the beginning of the work as far as 3.7; now with greater attention to details (the fragrance of the bridegroom is symbolic of the generation of the Logos; the darkness of the bride is symbolic of her past sins; the walls and the roof of the house are symbolic of the patriarchs and the prophets, the foxes represent heretics (CSCO 264, 26, 31, 37f., 40)). The tone of the work suggests a sermon.

The series of *Blessings* represents Hippolytus' most ambitious and most successful exegetical undertaking. To evaluate it properly, we must bear in mind that alongside the *Blessings of Jacob*, relating to Gen. 49, and the *Blessings of Moses*, relating to Deut. 33, there was also the *Blessings of Balaam*, now lost, relating to Num. 23-24, and that the *Blessings of Jacob* does not confine itself to the interpretation of Gen. 49, but integrates this passage with Gen. 37 (Joseph's dreams), Gen. 27 (Isaac's blessing of Jacob), and Gen. 48 (Jacob's blessing on the sons of Joseph).

Hippolytus had oral traditions about Jacob's blessing of his sons, the star of Jacob in Num. 24:17ff.; the conflict between Isaac and Esau; and Joseph, all passages which had already been interpreted christologically. He highlighted the affinity which connects these passages of clear prophetic significance. For this reason he brought them together in a homogeneous group, either extending the basic typology to further passages, or else proposing a precise interpretation of all (or nearly all) the details of the various texts in a strictly christological manner, and more specifically in reference to the incarnation of Christ. His interpretation of Gen. 27:27 depends on Irenaeus, but where the latter had given an eschatological interpretation of the passage, Hippolytus looks for a more directly christological sense (PO 27, 8ff.). The theme which he develops most here, is that of the substitution of Christians in place of the Jews as beneficiaries of God's promises. It is in this sense that he interprets episodes which show a younger brother prevailing over the first-born: Jacob and Esau, Ephraim and Manasseh, Judah and Reuben.

Hippolytus' systematic exegesis signals a noteworthy step
forward in the history of patristic interpretation of Scripture,
compared to the more 'episodic' exegesis of Justin, Irenaeus
and Tertullian. Yet, it is precisely in the systematic character
that certain serious limitations can be seen. First of all, there
is a total lack of philological qualification, a criticism which
cannot be rejected as anachronistic when one considers the
progress made in this area by the Greeks and the Jews. When
Hippolytus briefly touches on the refusal of the Jews to
include the 'Susanna episode' in the Book of Daniel, he
adduces only motives of a purely moral kind, and seems to be
unaware that no Hebrew text of the episode was known, but
only a Greek translation (SC 14, 96).

Considering next his specific interpretative technique,
Hippolytus bases his christological typology on the traditional
conviction that the Old Testament conceals, under the literal
sense, the mysteries of Christ (PO 27, 2, 22, 42). These the
exegete has to uncover, with the help of the same Christ, who
thus becomes the revealer of his own mysteries (PO 27, 2).
The proven truthfulness of the prophets validates this
hermeneutical procedure (PO 27, 42). But given this
superimposition of two levels of reading, Hippolytus never
troubles to establish the relationship between them. In the
Commentary on Daniel, he has no difficulty in superimposing
the allegorical interpretation of Susanna on the literal,
developing it with particular attention to show up the rejection
of the Jews. In the *Commentary on the Song of Songs*, given the
particular nature of the text as a love song, the problem of the
literal meaning does not even arise.

However, the problem does arise in the *Blessings*, because
the reality of the patriarchical events cannot be called into
question. But now Hippolytus sees these events only in terms
of the hidden, christological significance which they had
from the beginning, and which alone permits the proper
evaluation of their true significance (PO 27, 160). For
Hippolytus, this means that certain events, certain words,
have their full sense only if considered in the light of Christ,
while their integrity at the literal level leaves something to be
desired. This, then, is the reason for his total lack of concern

for the literal meaning of these matters, and also for the extent to which he applied his criterion of reviewing incongruities in the literal meaning of the text which pointed to allegory. He reiterates Irenaeus' objections to the literal interpretation of the blessing of Isaac. He rejects the obvious literal application of the words of Jacob to Reuben, Simeon and Levi. He gives an absurd reading of Gen. 49:25-26: 'Blessings of breasts, blessings of the womb of your father and mother' instead of: 'blessings of breasts and womb, blessings of your father and mother' in order to produce an allegorical interpretation with a doctrinal meaning from the self-contradiction of 'father's womb' (PO 27, 24ff., 54ff., 60ff., 108f.). And yet, in the context of such a rigorously christological interpretation, he unexpectedly allows a partial reference to Samson in the Blessing of Dan (Gen. 49:16-18) (PO 27, 90) i.e. a Jewish interpretation. And in order to explain why Moses fails to bless in Deut. 33, Hippolytus refers indiscriminately to deeds of the patriarch, of the tribe, and of Christ (PO 27, 155ff.).

The lack of precise rules can also be seen in his interpretation of details: only occasionally are numbers interpreted symbolically (SC 14, 166; CSCO 264, 8); only once is interpretation based on the etymology of a Hebrew name, Asher = riches (PO 27, 96). On more than one occasion, the exegete finds himself in difficulties with some details of the text. Gen. 49:7: 'I will divide them in Jacob, I will scatter them among Israel' is interpreted giving improbable instrumental force to the preposition 'in' (PO 27, 66f.). Sometimes within a maze of fairly elementary typologies, a few more complicated examples stand out with excessive precision of material detail, e.g. in Gen. 49:21, the Blessing of Naphtali, the vine becomes the Saviour; the vine leaves, the saints; the clusters of grapes, the martyrs; the harvesters, the angels; the baskets, the apostles; the wine-press, the church; the wine, the power of the Holy Spirit (PO 27, 98).[24]

The pioneering nature of Hippolytus' exegetical work has deserved to be illustrated with some attention; indeed these works exhibit most fully both the strengths and the limitations of Asiatic exegesis.

NOTES

1. It should be remembered that *halakhah* could also be based, not in Scripture, but purely in tradition.

2. The Greek translation of the Old Testament known as the Septuagint was sometimes very free and interpretative.

3. The most complete text of this type which has survived is the *pesher* of Habakkuk.

4. These terms are attested rather late (1st cent. BC); earlier, the same concept was indicated by the term *hyponoia.*

5. The Messianic parable of the wicked husbandmen (Matt. 21:33ff.) is presented as a *Midrash* on Is. 5:1; Ps. 117:22-23.

6. Cf. Rom. 5:14. The prefiguration is an 'anti-type' in the sense that both Adam and Christ so sum me up in themselves all of humanity: Adam in sin, but Christ in salvation.

7. The early exegetes, even if they display a certain reserve about the use of the term *allegoria* and its cognates, do not distinguish between allegory and typology, and they consider spiritual interpretation as a type of allegorical interpretation, alongside the 'moral' interpretation, and so on. Modern scholars for the most part prefer to distinguish the two, inasmuch as typology has a historical basis in the activity of Christ or the Church, which is lacking in pagan allegory. Thus authors such as Clement, Origen, et al., see allegories of the moral or anagogical type, etc., against the traditional typologies, because they lack a historical foundation, and have non-Christian origins. Here we prefer to keep to the earlier usage and to consider typological (= spiritual) interpretation of the Old Testament as a type of allegorical interpretation, intending by 'allegory' the interpretative procedure (saying one thing and signifying another) and by 'typology' the contents of the allegorical interpretation (the Old Testament, 'typos' of the New Testament).

8. This work in its definitive edition dates back to the late 4th century, but it uses much older material (2nd/3rd century).

9. Ps.-Barnabas uses the term *typos* several times, but never *allegoria.*

10. From what has been said it is clear that literal and typological interpretations of the Old Testament cannot be categorically distinguished as belonging, respectively, to Jewish Christians and to the Christians of a Hellenistic background, since both tendencies were already represented in the Jewish-Christian world.

11. Origen, *De Princ.* II 5, 1 reports some of these episodes (the flood, the destruction of Sodom and Gomorrah, etc.) from which the Gnostics made out that the God of the Old Testament was just, but not good, unlike the God of the New Testament. The strict opposition between the two Testaments and between the just God of the one and the good God of the other, was also characteristic of Marcion (whom the ancients also considered a Gnostic), while modern scholars are less sure about categorising him in this way. In contrast to the Gnostics, Marcion would not recognise allegorical interpretation of Scripture. Given that the Gnostic rejection of the Old Testament originated in the opposition between the supreme God and the Demiurge, a lesser emphasis of this opposition might make it possible for the Old Testament to be used by the Gnostic in the same way as the New Testament. This is the case with the *Pistis Sophia and the Exegesis of the Soul.*

[12.]Cf. for example, Irenaeus, *Adv. Haer.* I 30:6-7, and for further documentation, my own 'Note sull'interpretazione gnostica dell Antico Testamento', *Vetera Christianorum* 9 (1972) 352ff. A fundamental characteristic of the Gnostic Demiurge, i.e. his ignorance of a divine world superior to himself, has its scriptural basis in Is. 45:5: 'I am the Lord, and there is no other, besides me there is no God.'

[13.]In the text in question, the interpretation of these individuals, which I list in the order in which they appear, is not always coherent: Cain, Esau and Nimrod were indeed the enemies of God, i.e. the Demiurge, but not Jacob and Joseph.

[14.]Indeed, Ps.-Barnabas, who was the first to propose the typology (see above) only considered the Joshua of Ex. 17:9ff. and Num. 13:1ff. Justin, on the other hand, bases his typology on the Book of Joshua itself: as he had led the people into the land of Canaan, so Christ leads Christians into the true promised land.

[15.]Strictly speaking, the cave is not mentioned in the Gospels, which only speak of a manger, but it became integral to popular tradition about the birth of Jesus through the connection of Is. 33:16 (which mentions a *spelaion*) with the Gospel account.

[16.]The Eve/Mary typology, which Irenaeus takes from Justin, is also highly developed compared with the original (V 19:1).

[17.]We should remember that Justin also wrote against Marcion, and here his interpretation of the Old Testament had to take account of its rejection by the heretic.

[18.]This term is commonly used by Justin. In a passage in a work now lost (quoted by Irenaeus, *Adv. Haer.* V 26:2), he also makes use of the term *allegoria*.

[19.]For the allegorising interpretation of the parable of the wicked husbandmen (Matt. 21:33ff.), see *Adv. Haer.* IV 36:2.

[20.]Theophilus' one concern is to make it clear that the one who walked in Paradise and spoke with Adam, was not God the Father, but his Son, the Logos, the subject of all the Old Testament theophanies.

[21.]Recently, Hippolytus of Rome has again been proposed as the author of this homily.

[22.]Given the uncertainty which persists over the historical and literary activity of this person, I should explain that my concern here is with the author of the exegetical writings to be examined later. I think this author to be an Eastern bishop, whom I distinguish from Hippolytus of Rome. For further information on this subject cf. *Ricerche su Ippolito*, Rome, 1977, p. 9ff., 151ff.

[23.]Cf. with SC 14, 72, the concern to provide a clear exposition of the historical events (see also p. 78). On p. 97, Hippolytus observes that Scripture shows us, for our instruction, both good and bad human actions.

[24.]For a detailed description of the ship/Church symbolism, see *De Antichr.* 59.

Chapter 2

Scripture in the Alexandrian Milieu

With respect to what had gone before, the cultural initiative of the so-called Alexandrian School tended towards a greater openness to the values of Greek 'paideia', with the particular intention of deepening the interpretation of Scripture, to make it more easily accessible to readers with a high level of education. The initiative was thus parallel to that undertaken much earlier by Philo and other Hellenised Jews, but now the immediate goal was to oppose the cultural predominance of the Gnostics and their interpretation of Scripture. The latter, as we have seen, interpreted the Old Testament in such a way as to underline the hiatus which separated it from the New Testament, and on the other hand, interpreted the New Testament by distorting its meaning in order to confirm the basic teachings of the Gnostics. It was precisely this long-lasting polemic with the Gnostics, over and above the contact with the superior cultural level of Hellenised Judaism, which stimulated a refinement in the exegetical technique of the catholic scholars at Alexandria, making them sensitive to requirements previously neglected by Asiatic exegesis, and equipping them to meet them.

Exegesis here both continued and further broadened the scope of the traditional typological interpretation of the Old Testament, and integrated this with the contribution of other forms of interpretation, especially that represented by Philo, i.e. the cosmological and anthropological interpretation of the Old Testament. To this were added more or less esoteric apocalyptic expectations, relating mainly to angelic powers. It would be superfluous to add that the favoured hermeneutical approach was allegorical. Given that we know almost nothing of Pantaenus, for us the exegesis of the Alexandrian School is represented, between the end of the 2nd century and the first half of the 3rd, by Clement and Origen.

1. *Clement*

In the now almost entirely lost *Hypotyposeis*, Clement, according to Eusebius (*HE* VI 14:1), presented summary expositions of the whole of Scripture, even of Books of doubtful canonicity. The little which has survived, touching in fact on some of the disputed letters of Peter, Jude and John in a Latin translation which may not be totally trustworthy, confirms the accuracy of Eusebius' claim; and some points of angelology and anthropology confirm the judgment of Photius (*Bibl.* 109), who charges Clement with having dealt in his work with the most varied doctrinal matters, with results which he considered erroneous. Fortunately, Clement's other extant writings, while not specifically exegetical, quote and discuss innumerable biblical texts and often also discuss hermeneutical theory. From such material we can form a fairly precise idea of Clement's scriptural concerns.

Clement, who regards Scripture as the actual voice of the divine Logos (*Protr.* 9:82, 84), takes up what was by now the traditional idea that the Gospel is the realisation and fulfilment of the Law and that, as a result, the Old Testament should be interpreted in the light of Christ (*Strom.* IV 21:134). He speaks, anti-Gnostically, of one single Testament, which has come to us from the one God through the mediation of the one Lord (*Strom.* II 6:29). While it may be true that the prophets and the apostles did not have a philosophical training, the use of this discipline can still help us to understand their words more fully. In fact, 'The Lord expressed himself in a mysterious way, so that not all might be able to understand what he says' (*Strom.* I 9:45). Indeed, Clement was convinced, with Philo, that Scripture cannot contain anything banal, and that every word was written with a precise intention. He was further convinced that this intention may be hidden, not immediately perceptible (*Strom.* IV 25:160): 'Do not throw your pearls before swine' (Matt. 7:6), because it is dangerous to explain perfectly pure and clear words about the true light to hearers as coarse and unlearned as pigs (*Strom.* I 12:55). Here the use of the word 'hearers', shows us that Clement thought in terms of a direct method of teaching, i.e. master to pupil, and that he considered the book by itself to be an unsatisfactory substitute. Thus the words of Christ appear to Clement to be an expression of a divine and mysterious wisdom, and we ought not to listen to them with a merely fleshly ear (*Quis Dives Salvetur* 5:2). The teachings of Scripture are divided into two levels, one for immediate understanding, and the other expressed in an obscure, concealed way, which rewards only the one who knows how to interpret it (*Paed.* III 12:97). Indeed, neither the prophets nor Our Lord himself expressed the divine mysteries in a simple way which would be accessible to all, but they spoke in parables (i.e. by allegories) as the apostles themselves declared (Matt. 13:34).

There were various reasons for this: to encourage the more zealous to sustained and skilful research, and because those who are not sufficiently prepared would receive more injury than help from a knowledge of Scripture. The sacred mysteries are reserved for the elect; those predestined for this 'gnosis'. This explains the characteristic use of the parable-style in Scripture (*Strom.* VI 15:124).

From all this, it becomes only too clear that such a conception of God's word and of its understanding could not but favour allegorical interpretation. Indeed, Clement not only adopted *allegoria* and related terms (*parabole, ainigma,* etc.) without the slightest hesitation, but in *Strom.* V 4:20ff. he has given us what is in effect a treatise on allegory and symbolism, understood as the characteristic expression of religious language. By its nature, this cannot be accessible to all, but requires certain purification and prohibitions. Clement presents this esoteric principle as having universal application in religious practice, and he illustrates his point by reference to the ideographic scriptures of the Egyptians, as an example of symbolic expression in religious language. In this way, allegory becomes the hermeneutical principle by which the teaching of Scripture is divided into two levels, as we saw earlier. The application of this principle allows us to pass from the lower, literal level to the higher, and so to penetrate the less obvious aspects of the teaching. Clement is not unaware of the risks involved in the application of this rule, and the excesses of Gnostic allegories plainly demonstrated this. Thus he observes that truth is found, not by changing the meaning of the text, because this could distort every truth, but only if the interpretation of a passage leads to a result which is appropriate and perfectly consonant with the majesty of God, and if it is based on the support of other biblical passages (*Strom.* VII 16:96). Only after discussing the use of Scripture as a norm for distinguishing orthodoxy from heresy, does Clement, like Irenaeus, enunciate the criterion of the antiquity of Catholic tradition compared with that of the heretics (*Strom.* VII 16:95).

In a difficult passage (*Strom.* I 28:176, 179), Clement divides the Law into four parts: the historical part, the legislative part (both are connected with ethical teaching), the part concerned with religious ceremonies (which corresponds to the natural sciences), and the fourth part, superior to the others, the theological part, the *epopteia*.[1] After a lengthy development he concludes that there are various ways of understanding the intention of the Law. Either it shows us a model, or it presents us with a symbol, or it imposes a command, or it makes a prophetic prediction. Without going into a complicated examination of details it is clear that Clement is proposing various ways of reading and understanding the sacred text. He does not disregard the basic, historical dimension of the text, and he is able to produce a doctrinal sense from it; yet, clearly his interest was in what he defined as *epopteia*: the hidden and mysterious meaning which is revealed only to the one who can interpolate the text in the right way, i.e. using allegorical interpretation.

This can take various forms. On the one hand, Clement continues to use the traditional typology, underlining the unity of the two Testaments in opposition to the Gnostics, as touched on earlier, and developing the concept of progressive revelation, according to which the coming of the Saviour was prepared from the beginning of the world; announced, indicated by word and deed in the Law and the prophets, and finally by John the Baptist (*Strom.* VI 18:166-167). Clement, who was greatly influenced by Philo, could adopt Philo's suggestions in a christological direction. In *Plant.* 169f., Philo had interpreted Gen. 26:8 (Abimelech sees Isaac through a window embracing Rebecca) on the basis of the etymology of Isaac (= laugher) and Rebecca (= patience), and took it to mean that the wise man (Abimelech) finds delight in wisdom. Clement (*Paed.* I 6:22-23) takes the passage, on the basis of the same etymologies as meaning Christ (= Abimelech) through the incarnation (= window) contemplates the joy and the constancy of the Church.

But the contribution of Philo is particularly apparent in 'cosmological' and 'moral' interpretation to which Clement gives much attention. He takes the Temple, for example, to be a symbol of the universe (*Strom.* V 6:32ff.) in a complex context in which various kinds of readings alternate, some typological (the candelabra is a 'typos' of Christ [6:35]). Even the tablets of the Law containing the Decalogue become a symbol of the world which contains ten elements: sun, moon, stars, clouds, light, wind, water, air, darkness and fire (*Strom.* VI 16:133). As an example of the 'moral' (i.e. psychological) type of interpretation, it will suffice to recall *Strom.* I 3:30-31, in which Abraham represents faith; Sarah, wisdom; Hagar, pagan culture; and the fact that Sarah gives birth to her son after Hagar signifies the contribution of Greek learning to the progress of true wisdom. The description of the entry of the High Priest into the Holy of Holies (Lev. 16:2ff.) inspired Clement to a complex allegory influenced by Philo: the golden breastplate which the High Priest removed after passing through the second veil, symbolises the body which, now purified (= gold), is abandoned by the soul in the intelligible world (= second veil) with the angels appointed to divine service (= at the altar of incense): *Exc. ex Theod.* 27.

These few examples are enough to show how far the straightforward allegorical interpretation of the Old Testament in Irenaeus and Hippolytus had become complex with Clement. It would be superfluous to go into the detail of an interpretative technique which, continuing in the steps of Philo, fully exploits the symbolism of numbers, the etymology of Hebrew names and other typically Alexandrian procedures far beyond the more frugal usage customary in the Asiatic School. But we must also recognise that, notwithstanding the impressive borrowing from Philo's exegesis, Clement dissociates himself fundamentally from Philo in that his interpretation of the Old Testament remains solidly anchored in Christ, i.e. in history.

2. *Origen*

If they are taken one by one, almost all the characteristics of Origen's exegesis, from the distinction of several messages in Scripture to the allegorical evaluation of the etymology of Hebrew names and the symbolism of numbers, can be found in exegetes who preceded him (especially Clement). But compared to his predecessors, Origen organised and systematised these more or less traditional features, using an incomparably superior knowledge of the actual biblical text, a far greater depth of exegetical reflection, and an unprecedented critical intelligence sharpened by debate with the Gnostics. He not only widened and deepened all that he received, but he ordered it, for the first time on precise methodological criteria, into a total synthesis which would in many ways remain definitive. In short, Origen made biblical hermeneutics into a real science, and, in that sense, he conditioned decisively all subsequent patristic exegesis.

Approaching his exegetical work from the more external data, we notice from the outset how he broadened the scope of Christian exegesis of Scripture, in terms both of form and subject. This is true of subject, because before him exegetes preferred to concentrate on a few Old Testament books (Genesis, Exodus, Psalms, Isaiah and little else), and systematically only on parts of these, as we have seen in Hippolytus. For the New Testament, the object of study was almost solely Matthew, certain letters of Paul, and in Millenarian milieux, the Book of Revelation. Origen, by contrast, understands the study of Scripture to mean the study of the whole of Scripture. He was the first to draw attention to certain Books of the Wisdom literature (Ecclesiastes, Job); his exegesis of Joshua and Judges has remained almost unparalleled in early exegetical literature. It is also true of form, because as far as we know, no-one before him had made a commentary in any systematic way on an entire book either of the Old Testament or the New Testament. The most ambitious attempt, represented by the 'Blessings' of Hippolytus, only covers about 100 verses in all, and both Hippolytus' or Heraclaeon's interpretation is given in a condensed, not to say summary fashion. Origen, on the other hand, set about making commentaries on entire books either of the Old or New Testament, even the entire Psalter. His interpretations could be unusually extensive: twelve books just for the first chapters of Genesis; thirty-three for John's Gospel and so on. We might recall in this context that Origen's exegetical work took different forms, early distinguished as: 'Scholia', 'Homilies' and 'Commentaries'. 'Scholia' were collections of explanations for selected passages chosen from this or that book after the pattern of the *Quaestiones* of Philo and similar works; 'Homilies' were preached at Caesarea before the gathering of the whole church community, and were therefore adapted in form and length to the requirements of a mixed and predominately uneducated congregation. These, however, do not have the typically rambling character of 'occasional' sermons, because Origen liked to give continuous cycles of homilies, preaching systematically on the more important episodes of entire Books. 'Commentaries' represent the specifically academic aspect of Origen's exegetical activity where the master could deepen his research without restriction of time or space in an exegesis which would try to explain a text exhaustively, in considerations and observations which would often carry the discussion far from its starting-point. In this the commentaries resemble those of Philo and those in vogue in the Greek philosophical schools.[2]

Origen's initial approach to the sacred text was philological. He was aware of arguments which arose in discussions with the Jews from variations in the biblical texts used by the two sides – we met something of this type earlier in dealing with Justin. Neither was he unaware that the Gnostics sometimes modified the sacred text to square it better with their own doctrines. Above all, he particularly felt the need to base his interpretation of Scripture, the Word of God, on preliminary research which would fix this word precisely. This need produced the 'Hexapla', a harmony of the Hebrew text and the Greek translations of the Old Testament[3] which marks an epoch in the study of Scripture. Even in the area of the Septuagintal text alone, Origen is concerned to compare manuscripts, and to identify and discuss variants. To illustrate Origen's precision in this critical research, it is enough to recall his reading of 'Bethabara' instead of 'Bethany' in John 1:28. Even if this does not convince us today, it is nonetheless based on a remarkable demonstration of coherent methodology and on the inspection which Origen claims to have made of that area of Palestine, in order to clarify uncertainty at first hand (*Comm. in Jo.* VI 40). The authority of his amendment was such that the reading 'Bethabara' crept into some manuscripts of John's Gospel.

Origen has also left a substantial theoretical treatise on Scripture and its interpretation in *De Princ.* IV 1-3, and this is the appropriate starting-point for outlining the fundamental characteristics of his hermeneutics. He does not limit himself to thinking of Scripture as a book inspired by the Holy Spirit, but as the divine word he effectively identifies it with Christ (= the Logos), the Word of God: the letter of the sacred text functions, like the human body assumed by Christ, as the envelope which encloses the divine Logos (*C. Celsum* VI 77; *Comm. Ser. in Mt.* 27): Sacred Scripture is the permanent incarnation of the Logos. Origen demonstrates its inspired character, by first treating it as a purely historical document: he allows his attention to rest on certain Old Testament passages, traditionally held to be messianic prophecies (Gen. 49:10; Deut. 32:21; etc.) and he shows how these prophecies were actually fulfilled in the human person of Christ (*De Princ.* IV 1:3ff.). In particular, he makes a point of showing that the extraordinary and irresistible diffusion of Christianity, in spite of every difficulty, even violent resistence, had already been predicted by Christ, and from this he deduces the divinity of Christ himself and also the divinely inspired character of his scriptures (*De Princ.* IV 1:2).

Origen treats as a traditional article of faith the belief that Scripture, over and above the literal sense, has a deeper spiritual sense which escapes the majority of people (*De Princ.* I, *Praef.* 8). Moreover, the difficulty in penetrating this sense was actually intended by the Holy Spirit to prevent profound truths from being too readily available to those unworthy of them, people who would not know how to appreciate them, since they would have been attained without any effort (*De Princ.* IV 2:7).[4] Indeed, the study of the sacred text demands not just application of thought, but a total personal commitment on the ascetic and moral level, something which earns for the scholar the indispensible help of God. The Spirit who inspired the sacred writers also inspires the interpreter (*De Princ.* IV 2:7; II 7:2).

The difficulty in understanding fully the meaning of God's Word thus lies in the fact that its deeper, essential and spiritual meaning is concealed beneath the literal expression which covers it, and clothes it like a veil, a garment, or a body (*De Princ.* III 6:1; IV 1:6; IV 2:8). This difficulty has caused many to stop at the level of the external, 'fleshly' sense, and they fall into error; the literal meaning though not itself mistaken does not represent the ultimate goal of Scripture, but serves rather, as an educative starting-point which points the reader to an awareness of the deeper meaning. If this awareness remains defective, error results – as with the Jews, who limited themselves to a merely material observance of the Law; or with the Gnostics, who took the anthropomorphisms of the Old Testament at face value, as do many of the less educated in the Church (*De Princ.* IV 2:1).

This distinction between the literal and spiritual meaning is developed by Origen, who extends the spiritual interpretation to every passage of the sacred text,[5] and distinguishes different types of spiritual meaning (*De Princ.* IV 2:4; IV 3:5) following influences from different directions: traditional typology, cosmological and anthropological exegesis in the style of Philo, a tendency, found not only in the Gnostics, to understand the earthly realities mentioned in Scripture 'vertically', as symbols of heavenly realities. To organise these different strands, Origen in *De Princ.* IV 2:4 makes a threefold division of the meanings of Scripture, parallel to the Pauline division of the human person into spirit, soul and body, or the division of Christians into *simpliciores (incipientes), progedientes,* and *perfecti.* Body / soul / spirit / corresponds to literal sense / moral sense / spiritual (or mystical) sense and to *incipientes / progredientes / perfecti.*[6]

But the application of this hermeneutical criterion is anything but systematic in Origen's exegetical work, and elsewhere he proposes a simpler distinction of the meanings of Scripture based on the identification of Scripture with Christ. The distinction between Christ as man and Christ as God corresponds to the distinction between the literal and spiritual sense of Scripture (*Hom. in Lev.* 1:1). This correlation is also extended to the more common distinction, which Origen introduces between simple and perfect Christians: Christ as man / Christ as God corresponds to literal meaning / spiritual meaning and to simple / perfect (*Comm. Ser. in Mt.* 27) in the sense that while simple, ignorant Christians will stop at the knowledge of the humanity of Christ and a literal understanding of Scripture, the perfect[7] rise to a knowledge of the divinity of Christ and the spiritual sense of Scripture. In effect, Origen often distinguishes two senses in his scriptural interpretations, the literal and the spiritual, which centred on Christ, can take various forms, as we shall see.

The distinction of two or three senses in Scripture shows us that these schematisations had only a relative value for Origen, compared with the fundamental and much more profound concept which underpinned the process. For him, the Word of God is inexhaustibly rich and the human reader cannot exhaust its meaning (*Comm. in Mt.* XIV 6); but as a seed produces more or less fruit in proportion to the industry of the farmer and the quality of the soil, so the mysteries of God's Word are uncovered in proportion to the application and the capacity of the exegete (*Hom. in Ex.* 1:1). In fact, Origen sees the relationship between the sacred text and its reader not statically, as the passive apprehension of something given, but dynamically as an effort by the exegete to penetrate ever more deeply into the inexhaustible depths of God's Word, according to his own skill and tenacity. The meanings of God's Word are infinite, and so are the levels in which the reader can progressively share as he grows in spiritual fitness.

* * *

When we come to examine more closely the various senses which Origen distinguishes in Scripture, we should first note that Origen, whose name is a byword for the use of allegory, is also the same person who gave much more weight than ever before to the literal sense; and even if on the one hand, he criticises the *simpliciores* for stopping at this level, he is capable on the other hand of integrating it into an organic system of interpretation. Apart from the statements in *De Princ.* IV 2:6 and IV 3:4, it will suffice to recall here that while Hippolytus gave a purely typological (i.e. spiritual) interpretation to the Song of Songs, Origen in his Commentary systematically prefaces this interpretation with a literal one, designed to reconstruct the manner in which the action between the bride and bridegroom unfolds. To understand the reason for this approach, we need to go back both to the need to refute the excessive allegorisation of the Gnostics (which is why Origen maintains that correct interpretation must make the connection between the letter and the spirit of the sacred text, *De Princ.* IV 2:9; IV 3:4); to our author's Platonising cast of mind which applies to the interpretation of Scripture the distinction between sensible reality (= the literal sense) and imtelligible reality (the spiritual sense).

To the extent that sensible reality is an image and reflection of intelligible reality he sees it as a point of departure enabling one to pass from the lower to the higher level of understanding. Thus the literal sense, with its educative function, has a precise though modest value in the interpretative procedure.

The literal sense, as we have just said, is of 'modest value' – so modest that Origen often quite willingly denies its presence in certain scriptural contexts. The procedure is not new: we have already noticed it in Hippolytus, in Philo and in the philosophical exegesis of the Homeric poetry, and we have also seen the reasons for it: to eliminate, through allegorical interpretation, passages too crudely anthropomorphic in their representation of divinity, which disconcerted educated Greeks and encouraged the rejection of the Old Testament by Gnostics. This hermeneutical criterion was incorporated by Origen as an integral part of his theory of scriptural exegesis: 'With regard to Scripture as a whole, we are disposed to admit that all of it has a spiritual significance, but not all of it has a literal significance, since in several places it can be seen that a literal sense is impossible' (*De Princ.* IV 3:5).[8] God himself arranged that the Old Testament should include improbable or scandalous passages to lead the interpreter to search for a deeper meaning (IV 2:9). Origen is, if anything, over-zealous in the application of this criterion, not just to the obvious anthropomorphisms of the early chapters of Genesis (God 'planting' the garden of Eden, and 'walking' in the garden, Gen. 2:8; 3:8) and similarly improbable situations (the devil leading Jesus up a mountain from which he could see all the kingdoms of the world, Matt. 4:8); but also where the sacred text expresses itself in a metaphorical or imaginative way, e.g. the gospel instructions to greet no-one on the way, or not to have two tunics (Lk. 10:4; Matt. 5:39) (*De Princ.* IV 3:1-3)). Clearly with this 'hyper-literalism' Origen multiplies the difficulties attached to the letter of the sacred text, precisely in order to facilitate the transition to a spiritual reading. This interpretative criterion finds an application of particular historical significance in Rev. 21 (the New Jerusalem coming down to earth from heaven) and with prophetic texts which celebrate the richness of the future messianic era – all texts which millenarians took at face value. Origen reproached them for abandoning all intellectual effort, and for sticking solely to the literal sense of Scripture. He himself interprets all these passages spiritually, i.e. allegorically: e.g. the precious stones of the New Jerusalem are the saints, and so on (*De Princ.* II 11:2-3). Thus he deprives the millenarians of the scriptural basis of their teaching.

Apart from using real or presumed deficiencies in the literal sense, to move on to the allegorical sense,[9] Origen also employs all the typical procedures of the Alexandrian tradition; not only numbers and etymologies of Hebrew names, but a thousand details of the sacred text: (names of animals, plants, etc.) become opportunities for allegory. Yet, he was also aware of the risk of arbitrariness inherent in such procedures and tried to counter them in various ways: he emphasises that the literal sense is defective only in a few cases (*De Princ.* IV 3:4); he requires that the spiritual interpretation should be connected to the literal meaning and confirmed by other scriptural passages (IV 2:9; IV 3:4, 5). Refuting Heraclaeon's interpretation of John, he reproaches the Gnostics for an interpretation which is contradictory to its context and forces a point without any scriptural support – though he can still sympathise with some of their positions (*Comm. in Jo.* II 14, 21; VI, 60; XIII 10, 17, 60). Even if, to our eyes, much of Origen's interpretation of Scripture seems arbitrary, in terms of the criteria in use at the time, it in fact appears coherent.

As we have already observed, the content of Origen's allegorical interpretation is varied. In the last part of his theoretical treatise in *De Princ.* IV 1-3, he gives several examples of anagogical[10] interpretation, where earthly realities symbolise heavenly realities: Jerusalem, Israel, the Tribes, the surrounding nations, are all *typoi* of spiritual creatures who dwell in the heavens (IV 3:7-10). Origen is interested in this type of speculation because his anthropology is based on the idea that humans are in fact heavenly beings weighed down by a material body and fallen to earth as a result of their sin. He explains certain Scripture passages quoted in *De Princ.* IV 3:10-12 in this sense.

These interpretative directions, though well represented in the body of Origen's work, are not predominant. Much more attention is devoted to 'moral' interpretation, which has for its object the interior life of the Christian. Here we need to make a clear distinction between the different types of interpretation contained within this one kind: sometimes it may be a simple lesson in morality (*De Princ.* IV 2:6); sometimes it may be an anthropological interpretation in the style of Philo: Lot and his wife are respectively symbols of reason and sensuality (*Hom. in Gen.* 5:2). Most often, however, he individualises traditional typology, in the sense that he refers the sacred text to the relationship between the Logos and the soul of each Christian. Origen greatly enriched this area of traditional exegesis.

Where Hippolytus had interpreted the Song of Songs on a common Christ/Church typology, Origen, develops this by prefacing a literal reading to a spiritual interpretation which describes the relationship between the Logos and the soul: the perfect soul, that of the bride; still imperfect, that of the bridesmaids.

Origen was a great mystic, and his whole thinking on this subject was scripturally based: it will suffice to recall Homily 27 on the Book of Numbers, in which the various stages of the Israelites' journey through the desert are seen as the successive stages of the soul's ascent to God; the 'lovely tents' of Israel in Num. 24:5, being temporary dwellings, become a symbol of the one who grows endlessly in the knowledge of God (*Hom. in Num.* 17:4). The Gospel account of the Transfiguration (Matt. 17:1ff.) indicates the various ways in which Jesus can be known by the Christian (*Comm. in Mt.* XII 37).

The tendency to spiritualise allegory is also evident in Origen's typology. We noticed earlier how the Asiatic interpretation of the Passover referred the details of Exodus 12 to the concrete details of Jesus' passion. Origen, by contrast, gives them a spiritual significance, e.g. the period during which the lamb must be kept (Ex. 12:6) indicates that we can only eat the Passover (i.e. the mysteries of Christ), after adequate requisite moral progress (*Pasch.* 18). Indeed, he tends to deny that historical events can be *typoi* of other historical events; corporeal things are types of spiritual realities, and historical events are types of intelligible realities (*Comm. in Jo.* X 18).

As to the relationship between the Old Testament and the New Testament, Origen regularly bases it, anti-Gnostically, Heb. 8:5 and 10:1: the Old Testament presents the shadow and the image of truths which are fully revealed in the New. I give only one example, since the gradual progression Law / prophets / New Testament is connected with the distinction, already mentioned, between Christians as *incipientes* (= Law), *progredientes* (= prophets), *perfecti* (= New Testament) (*Hom. in Lev.* 1:4). But if Origen tends to emphasise the superiority of

the New Testament over the Old, he sometimes hesitates lest
an overemphasis in this direction should encourage the
Gnostics in their deprecation of the Old Testament. In these
cases he sees the advance of the New Testament over the Old
as quantitative. In the old dispensation, only a few – the
prophets, Moses, the patriarchs – understood the spiritual
meaning of the Law, i.e. the mysteries of Christ; now this
knowledge is for many (*De Princ.* II 7:1; *Comm. in Jo.* VI 4:6;
XIII 47-48).

In any case, the systematic christological interpretation
which Origen gives to the Old Testament leads him to take the
Old Testament and the New, i.e. the whole of Scripture
together, which some would take solely in a fleshly sense, and
others purely spiritually (*Comm. in Jo.* I 7; XIII 5-6).

Origen is carried all the more in this direction in that he
extends his typological interpretation to the New Testament.
Thus, using Heb. 10:1, Origen sometimes distinguishes the
Old Testament and New Testament as being, respectively, the
shadow and the image of heavenly realities (*Hom.* 38 *Ps.* 2:2).
Here, the typology is 'vertical', i.e. anagogical, but elsewhere it
is 'horizontal', in the sense that, as the Old Testament is the
typos of the New, so the New Testament is a *typos* of the 'eternal
gospel' of Rev. 14:6. As Christ at his first coming perfected the
Law, which presents the shadow of good things to come, so in
his coming in glory, he will bring to completion the shadow
represented by his first coming (*De Princ.* IV 3:13; *Comm. in Jo.*
I 7). The whole of salvation history is here laid out by Origen
distributed into three decisive periods with a clear projection
towards the eschatological stage, the time of the third Passover
(*Comm. in Jo.* X 18).

3. *The Spread of Alexandrian Exegesis*
We should consider both the difficulties in which Justin finds
himself in his evaluation of Christian interpolations in the Old
Testament, and Origen's public preaching on a Septuagintal
text corrected from variants in other Greek versions; both
Hippolytus' indifference to the critical and linguistic dimensions
of the Greek text of the Susanna episode, and the depth and
shrewdness with which Julius Africanus and Origen handle the

same passage, noticing word-play in the Greek text, the historical and social features of the story, and internal Old Testament quotations. It then is natural that Alexandrian hermeneutical criteria (substantially those of Origen) should have played such a part in the diffusion of Alexandrian culture, both in Egypt outside the immediate circles of this school, and even beyond Egypt. But this did not happen without opposition on the part of those who found such criteria over-innovative *vis-à-vis* tradition.

The lack of documentation allows us to focus, incompletely only on a single episode: the dispute between *Dionysius of Alexandria* and the millenarians of Arsinoe, following the account given by Eusebius (*HE* VII 24-25). The exegetical element was fundamental, because we have seen that Origen had given a scriptural interpretation to Rev. 21 and those other scriptural passages which, literally interpreted, constituted the very foundations of Millenarianism. Eusebius' résumé of *Against Allegorists* written by Nepos, the leader of the Millenarians, should be seen as an attempt to reject such an interpretation in favour of the traditional, literal one. We know nothing else about this work, and so we are unable to say whether the book attacked only the allegorical interpretation of texts relating to this debate, or whether it was extended to reject allegorical exegesis in general, as we have already seen radical Jewish Christians do.[11]

Perhaps Dionysius took Nepos' anti-Origenistic position into account when, dealing with the Book of Revelation, he followed a different critical approach, underlining the difficulty of the text, and suggesting the existence of a deeper meaning below the surface level. His own admission that he cannot understand it, emphasises indirectly (and not without a certain irony) the arrogance of the Millenarians in basing their doctrine upon so abstruse a text (*HE* VII 25:4-5). In this context, obviously with the aim of minimising the value of Revelation, Dionysius denies that it can have been written by the author of the Fourth Gospel. His observations, especially on the differences of style and language between the two works are still valuable, and constitute an initial confirmation of the level to which Origen had raised the study of Scripture.[12]

Nepos' anti-allegorical position would have been widely echoed in Asian circles, concerned to counter the spread of Alexandrian culture. But even in these areas Origen's exegesis exercised an influence.[13] Traces of this can be found, at the turn of the 3rd and 4th centuries, in Methodius of Olympus, notwithstanding his anti-Origenist position in defence of Millenarian eschatology. In any case, even the title of his *Symposium* suggests a sympathy for Plato, a proof of the variety of influences which were able to co-exist in these last representatives of an Asiatic school already in crisis. In this work, alongside touches of traditional typology, the influence of Origen can be detected, e.g. in the presentation of virgins as brides of the Logos, and in the gradation between virgins and other orders of Christians within the Church, following the Alexandrian's *Commentary on the Song of Songs* (*Symp.* 7:2, 3). His comparison of the ten virgins of the parable in Matt. 25:1ff., with the five senses, pure, or sullied by sin (6:3), is derived directly from Origen (*Comm. Ser. in Mt.* 63).

The most characteristic example of this convergence of diverse influences in Methodius can be found in *Symp.* 9:1, 5: here he cites Lev. 23:39ff. which lists the prescriptions for the feast of Tabernacles, and rebukes the Jews for having taken this text literally when taken allegorically, it prefigures the future resurrection of the body. The fact that the feast is celebrated in the seventh month of the year prefigures the time when the world will reach its fulfilment in the seventh millennium – the millennium of the rest of the righteous with Christ. The extraordinary nature of Methodius' procedure lies in his attempt to base his doctrine of the millennium on the allegorical interpretation of a Scripture passage, while reproaching the Jews for a literal interpretation (i.e. for precisely the kind of interpretation which Origen had criticised in the Millenarians). Methodius failed to see what Nepos saw clearly, namely that Millenarianism could only permit literal interpretation of certain Scripture passages. To interpret Lev. 23:39ff. allegorically, in an eschatological sense, as he does, amounted to inviting adversaries to propose similar interpretation of passages which Millenarians had to interpret literally. Clearly, Methodius did not manage to reconcile satisfactorily the diverse influences to which he was subject.

NOTES

1. The term comes from the language of pagan mystery cults, which Clement readily adopts to describe the realities of the Christian mystery. Clement glosses it with quotations from Plato and Aristotle.

2. Much of Origen's immense exegetical output has been lost, mostly because of repeated condemnations of him from the end of the 4th century onwards. In the original Greek we have books of his Commentaries on Matthew and John, and a collection of homilies on Jeremiah; in Latin translations by Jerome and Rufinus, we have Commentaries on the Song of Songs and on Romans, somewhat simplified in comparison with the originals and also collections of homilies on Luke and on various books of the Old Testament (Genesis, Exodus, Isaiah, Psalms, etc.). The Tura papyri have given us (in poor condition) a treatise on Easter; and there is much fragmentary material.

3. On six adjacent columns, Origen transcribed, following contemporary reconstructions, the Hebrew text in Hebrew characters, the Hebrew text transliterated into Greek, and the translations of Aquila, Symmachus, the Septuagint, and Theodosius. For the Psalms Origen added two anonymous translations which he found himself. The complete text of the Hexapla has not come down to us, so our knowledge is baed on extensive fragmentary material, pertaining mainly to the four columns of the Greek translations, which in early times were transcribed alone without the Hebrew Text (the Tetrapla).

4. Here and elsewhere Origen supports this concept by quoting or alluding to, Matt. 7:6 (do not throw your pearls before swine), a text which we have also seen Clement use in an analogous context.

5. The systematic way in which Origen interprets Scripture spiritually, i.e. allegorically, allows him to reproach even Heraclaeon for the literalism, and hence over-simplicity, of certain of his interpretations (*Comm. in Jo.* XII 41, 53, 60). He can thus reverse the charge of excessive simplicity which Gnostics commonly levelled at catholics.

6. Here and elsewhere Origen bases this concept on the quotation of Prov. 22:20 (?): 'write these concepts three times, in your soul and in your mind'. The sense of the threefold relationship lies in the requirement that each person and each part of every person should draw benefit from a knowledge of the sacred text.

7. Recall that for Origen, the term 'perfect' is always relative, applied to the Christian because the progress towards perfection is for him unending (*Hom. in Num.* 17:4).

8. God's command to Noah to build the ark with two or three decks (Gen. 6:16) is supposed by Origen to bolster his claim that Scripture usually has three senses, but sometimes only two, since the literal meaning is lacking (*Hom. in Gen.* 2:6).

9. It would be superfluous to emphasise that Origen habitually uses the term 'allegory'. In fact, the debate between pagans and Christians over the validity of allegorical interpretation concerned not so much the procedure itself and its related terminology, but its content. Celsus and Porphyry allegorised pagan myths, but held that the contents of the Bible were too simplistic and unrefined to mask a second meaning under the literal level, which might be interpreted allegorically. For his part, Origen allegorises Scripture, and objects to Celsus that myths cannot be allegorised because of their immoral content. On this, cf. J.

Pépin, *Mythe et allégorie*, Paris 1958, p. 447ff.

[10.]For Origen, who was the first to adopt the term exegetically, *anagoge* (= raising up) is substantially synonymous with 'allegory'. It later came to mean a 'vertical' type of allegory, in which earthly realities were symbols of heavenly ones. For convenience, we use the term here in this latter sense.

[11.]It was not by chance that Millenarianism rooted itself in a messianism understood in a purely Jewish way.

[12.]Eusebius (*HE* VI 25:11-13) quotes a passage from Origen in which he underlines the difference in style and composition between Hebrews and the Pauline letters, and he ascribes Hebrews to an editor who had expressed Pauline concepts in an original manner.

[13.]Some modern scholars have deduced that in Alexandria around the period of the episcopacy of Peter (end of the 3rd or the beginning of the 4th century), there was a reaction against Origen's exegesis. This is on the basis of early information about opposition to Origen's interpretation of Gen. 3:21 (the garments of skins worn by Adam and Eve after the Fall represent the material body which encases the soul). In fact, Peter was reacting only against the Platonic doctrine, taken up by Origen, of the pre-existence of souls in relation to bodies, and not against the criteria of Origen's exegesis in general. On this subject cf. 'Le origini dell arianesimo', *Rivista di storia e letteratura religiosa* 7 (1971), 321ff.

Chapter 3

The High Point of Exegetical Literature in the East

The new policy towards the Church begun by Constantine affected the development of exegetical literature, between the 4th and 5th centuries, as of every other type of literature. The great expansion of Christian religion, accompanied, generally speaking, by a lower level of preparation and conviction on the part of new initiates brought about the need to encourage greater familiarity with Scripture, both at the popular and at a more intellectual level, by means of both the homily and the commentary.

Origen's lead was decisive for both genres, whether by the systematic illustration of entire books of Scripture (or large portions of them) through integrated though long cycles of homilies, or by written commentaries which were just as systematic and thorough. Both the commentary, and sometimes, the homily, rested on a historical, archaeological, and linguistic training unknown in the Christian world before Origen.[1] In the homily, however, the objectives of moral teaching and edification often accompanied or overrode purely exegetical intentions (John Chrysostom, Ambrose, etc.), giving to preaching a character quite distinct from Origen's style of homily. What was quite in harmony with the Alexandrian's precedents in both genres was the great potential for doctrinal development, in relation to current debates, especially the Arian controversy. The threat of Manicheism revived the anti-Gnostic theme of the relationship between the Old and New Testaments, but with less vigour than before. But this danger does not seem to have been perceived at the same level everywhere. In the West especially, knowledge of the Old Testament was scant.

Origen's influence is widely seen, from East to West, both in form and in the actual content of interpretation. But in this context, apart from criticism of excessive allegorisms condemned even by Alexandrian exegetes (Didymus), there was now a reserve, not to say downright hostility, in the name of an appreciation of the sacred text which was orientated less towards allegory, and more towards the literal meaning of the text.

Behind this reaction there undoubtedly lay an uneasiness with the excesses of Alexandrian exegesis, the more so because Origen's successors did not share his mastery of the subject. Origen's allegorical interpretation of Scripture based its theoretical presuppositions on a Platonic interpretation of all reality. For his successors, as we shall see, it appeared to be more of an expedient, an arbitrary solution to certain difficulties posed by the literal level of the sacred text. Here we might remember that even in pagan circles, the allegorical interpretation of Homer and of myths in general encountered various forms of opposition;[2] and especially that Porphyry had recently charged the Christians, and Origen specifically, with arbitrary allegorisation of Scripture (Eusebius, *HE* VI 19:4-5). We know what a profound effect Porphyry's criticism had among the educated classes in Eastern Christianity. It is little wonder, then, that there was a preference in the Antiochene world for explaining the anthropomorphisms and other interpretations of Scripture by methods other than allegory: the sacred writer's accommodation to the low intellectual level of the Jews, the use of rhetorical devices, or of exaggerated or expressive modes of speech, and so on.

But alongside this obvious motivation for the anti-allegorising reaction, I believe we must look for another and profounder reason in a certain change of outlook and cultural interests which can be detected in educated Christian circles of the 4th and 5th centuries, now grown enormously. These interests, despite their impact on Scripture, are so to speak secular: historical, scientific, and archaeological. In other words, allegorical interpretation of Scripture allowed an entirely christological reading of the Old Testament, so that for Hippolytus, Origen and others, the historical vicissitudes of Israel or details of the biblical account of creation held no interest in themselves, apart from the connection they might have with Christ and the Church. But now, in certain circles an interest was taken in just these subjects for their own sake and hence also in a way of reading the text which was not simply christological (that is to say, allegorical), but which instead adhered more faithfully to the letter of the sacred text. It is superfluous to emphasise that such an approach, which gave precedence to a literal rather than an allegorical interpretation, found limited acceptance, as we shall see, while elsewhere the traditional method continued to hold sway. However, even where allegorical interpretation of the Old Testament persisted, there was a tendency to restrict considerably the scope of allegory in the interpretation of the New Testament, where the primary sense of the text set Christ and the Church before the reader, and hence where the excesses of allegory were more obvious.

1. *Eusebius*

Eusebius of Caesarea, reflecting both the persecuted Church and the Church of the Constantinian epoch, represents an important link between the old and new ways of interpreting Scripture. He was both a considerable authority on, and admirer of the works of Origen, which he had at his disposal in the library at Caesarea. And it was to Origen that he owed his insistence on critical and philological precision in handling the sacred text. As a young man he had worked with his master Pamphilus in transcribing and disseminating Origen's *Tetrapla* and particularly on the text of the Septuagint annotated with variants from other Greek translations. It was this text which he had constantly before his eyes when he was engaged in biblical interpretation, and he was capable of choosing among contrasting variants, and doing so differently from Origen. At the end of the introduction to the *Demonstratio Evangelica* (1:5) he underlines the differences between the various translations of the Old Testament, and declares his preference for the Septuagint, because this is the version employed by the Church, but he reserves the right to turn to other, more recent translations where it seems necessary for the purposes of a particular discussion.

The historical and archaeological interests of the author of the *Ecclesiastical History* and the *Chronicle* are fully apparent in the *Evangelical Canons*, a complex synopsis which allows the reader, starting from one Gospel, to find the parallel passages in the others and in the *Onomasticon*, a dictionary of the places mentioned in the Bible, with a short explanation of each. This is merely a small remnant surviving from a much larger work on the geography and topography of Palestine, which included a plan of Jerusalem and of the Temple.

The Jewish patriarchs especially, favoured by tradition as *typoi* of Christ, interested Eusebius as historical characters on whom one could establish the antiquity of the Christian tradition (*Preparatio Evangelica* VII 8; *HE* I 4:5ff.). Such an interest explains the evident diffidence of Eusebius as an exegete towards indiscriminate allegorical exegesis, but not, I think, entirely. We need to add to this his equally strong apologetic concerns, which, among other things recall the anti-Christian polemic of Porphyry. To present to pagans already on their guard due to controversy a heavily allegorised reading of the Old Testament was to lay oneself open to easy rejoinders – hence it was preferable to sacrifice quantity for quality and to be selective about the material one placed before readers of this kind.

Thus in the *Eclogae Propheticae* (c. 310), presenting a rich series of Old Testament passages with christological significance, Eusebius disregards those texts where christological reference is extracted from typology (e.g. Joseph, Joshua, and David, *typoi* of Christ) and instead chooses a few passages dealing with theophanies[3] and particularly, prophetic passages whose fulfilment in Christ could be demonstrated on the basis of a reading of the text that was spiritual but also immediate in that the text had never been given any meaning other than a christological one. To this end, Eusebius employs (but very sparingly), the traditional argument of a deficiency in the immediate literal sense, as in the case of Gen. 27:29 (the blessing of Jacob by Isaac), where he points out, following the lead of Irenaeus and Hippolytus, that those words were never fulfilled in Jacob and must therefore refer directly to Christ (I 6); and in connection with Is. 28:14-17, where Eusebius scorns a materialistic interpretation of the chosen stone which the Lord lays in the foundations of Sion, and refers the prophecy to Christ (IV 13). In this general context in which the christological interpretation of the Old Testament does not involve a systematic allegorical reading of the selected texts, Eusebius at times does indulge in specifically allegorical procedures in the interpretation of details: the Lebanon of Is. 10:34 symbolises Jerusalem (IV 8); the cloud of Is. 19: 1 ('The Lord is riding on a swift cloud') symbolises the flesh assumed by the Logos, and Egypt, the cloud's destination symbolises this human life (IV 10).[4]

Book I 4 of the *Eclogae Propheticae* is entirely devoted to the presentation of prophetic texts from Isaiah. We must recall that if Eusebius developed the prophetic argument of the Eclogues in an apologetic context in *Demonstratio Evangelica* II 5-10, he also devoted a proper commentary to the Book of Isaiah, which handles the whole book systematically. Jerome reproaches him (PL 24, 154, 179) that, after promising in the Introduction (which we no longer possess)[5] to interpret Isaiah historically, he more than once moves on to allegory after the criteria of Origen. In fact, Eusebius gives clear indications that he had Origen's major commentary on Isaiah to hand as he worked. Specific allegories[6] are common enough in this work: the cedars of Lebanon in Is. 2:13 are the demonic powers which rule the world; the clouds of the Is. 5:6 are the prophets; the growth of cypress and myrtle among brambles and nettles (Is. 55:13) symbolises the fertility of the soul which turns away from evil to good.[7] But Eusebius' commentary is quite different from Origen's purely allegorical approach: not only is the historical setting of the prophetic text amply developed, but the fulfilment of the prophecies in Christ is given as the first, immediate sense of the text: see the commentary on such famous passages as Is. 11:1ff., and 60:6ff. Particularly significant are certain programmatic remarks (cf. the beginning of the commentary and the commentary on Is. 11:15), in which Eusebius claims that the prophet has presented his message sometimes in a manner quite intelligible at the literal level and at other times using allegorical language. Here we encounter a significant departure from Origen, according to whom the spiritual sense (i.e. the allegorical one) is to be found throughout the whole of Scripture.[8]

The *Commentary on the Psalms*[9] reveals the same fusion of historical and apologetic interests: again passing over the *typoi* of the Old Testament in favour of the *logoi*, Eusebius can interpret very many of the Psalms as prophecies which have found effective fulfilment only in Christ, thus maintaining (save in a few cases) an interpretation of the sacred text on one level only, compared with the two or three of Origen's method. He pays particular attention to the historical background of the Psalms, referring continuously to events related in the historical or prophetic books.[10] In this way, he actually proposes a criterion for the ordering of the entire psalter (PG 23, 444ff.). The Psalms are structured in two blocks, respectively up to and after Ps. 50, in reverse chronological order, in that the first fifty are subsequent to the story of David and Bathsheba, while those after Ps. 50 refer to events which took place earlier: 'I believe,' observes Eusebius, 'that such an order was devised to prevent the theme from moving from better matters to worse.'

The christological reference is not systematically explored, so as not to force the sense of the text, but the number of christological psalms is still very high, always keeping in mind that sometimes only a few verses from the psalm are interpreted in this way (cf., for example, Ps. 85). Sometimes the christological interpretation is introduced without contrivance. Ps. 82, says Eusebius (1072), is entirely about the incarnation of Christ, in Ps. 86, the reference to Christ is only sketched out; in Ps. 87 it is quite clear (1052). At other times christological interpretation is based on the impossibility of referring the words of the psalm to the deeds of either David or Solomon: as in Pss. 54 and 71 (473, 789f.). At other times still, he follows the indications of the rubrics to the Psalms: the indication which accompanies the christological psalms 44, 68, 59, 79, 'for those who will be transformed', foretells the changes which the coming of Christ would provoke among Jews and Christians (553, 721). As already indicated, cases of a specifically allegorical reading of the text are rare: Babylon, Rahab, Tyre in Ps. 86:4 symbolise the call of the pagans (1048).

At the beginning of the commentary (73), Eusebius observes that everything is stored in the Psalter, as if in a large public storehouse. The notion that the Psalter was a kind of compendium of the whole Old Testament was to enjoy great success and would contribute to it becoming the most widely read book of the Old Testament, so attracting also the special attention of exegetes. The *Commentary* of Eusebius, full, but not excessive; christological, but not forced; historical, but not heavy; was compiled to meet of the tastes of the period, and achieved great prominence. It encapsulates the preference of the author for the Old Testament, compared with the New Testament which seems to have inspired his critical spirit only in the attempt to resolve the difficulties arising from the Gospel genealogies of Christ and the post-Easter appearances (*Quaestiones ad Stephanum / ad Marinum*). The profile given by Eusebius to the early roots of Christianity in the Old Testament, for apologetic purposes, led him to show the presence of Christ in the Old Testament, limiting his direct presentation of the New Testament period to brief preliminary references in the *Ecclesiastical History*.

2. *Syro-Palestinian Exegesis of the 4th Century: Origins of the School of Antioch*

In Eastern exegesis of the 4th and 5th centuries, the emergence of the so-called Antiochene school with a programme antagonistic to the allegorising exegesis of the Alexandrian school, is of fundamental importance. Modern scholars normally consider Lucian of Antioch as its founder, or at any rate, of Antiochene exegetical doctrine. Lucian was a priest martyred in 312. According to Jerome and others, he made a critical revision of the text of the Septuagint, displaying a concern for the letter of the text which underlay Antiochene exegetical practice. In fact, we know nothing of Lucian's specific exegetical activity, and the little information which we possess about him is so hard to interpret that it would be best to ignore the position which modern scholars have given him, and, locating the real beginning of the School as such with

Diodorus of Tarsus in the final decades of the 4th century, to probe for its origins in Syro-Palestinian exegesis of the preceding decades.

We have already commented upon a remarkable literalist tendency in Asian exegesis, alongside the traditional typology; we can be sure that this tendency was strengthened by the controversies which, between the second half of the 3rd and the start of the 4th century accompanied the spread of Alexandrian culture, of which the allegorical exegesis of Scripture was an important vehicle, into geographical areas which were then of an Asiatic cultural stamp. The convergence of Theophilus on one hand, and John Chrysostom on the other, on a literal interpretation of the first chapters of Genesis, shows the continuity of the literalist tradition in Antioch. In the first years of the 4th century Eustathius of Antioch, writing to refute the interpretation which Origen had given to the encounter between Saul and the witch of Endor (1 Sam. 28), accuses the Alexandrian of having allegorised all Scripture, giving allegorical readings of passages which ought to have been interpreted solely in a literal manner, and of using arbitrary procedures of suit his need, e.g. the abuse of etymologies of Hebrew names (PG 18, 656ff.).

But alongside this tencency of Asiatic origin, the influence of Eusebius can also be detected in Syro-Palestinian exegesis of the 4th century. As we have seen, while remaining a fervent supporter of Origen, he had re-proportioned the allegorism of his master's exegesis, while fully embracing his philological and critical skills, and himself adding an historical interest. The combination of these two tendencies paradoxically meant that it was precisely the influence of Origen's philology, textual criticism, and respect for the literal text, which gave methodological consistency to the early Asiatic literalism. This fostered a progression from the exegesis of Eustathius to that of Diodorus, quite differently constituted – at the expense of typically Alexandrian allegorical exegesis. And I have already touched more generally, at the beginning of this chapter, on the considerations which encouraged an attitude of reserve or even hostility to what was considered the excessive allegorism of the Alexandrians.[11]

Notwithstanding the lack of extant documentation, we can still reconstruct the confluence of these different motives in three exegetes who were active in the Syro-Palestinian area in the middle decades of the 4th century: Acacius of Caesarea, Eusebius of Emesa and Apollinaris of Laodicea. Their cultural background was different: Acacius was a disciple of Eusebius of Caesarea; Eusebius of Emesa was educated in Antioch at the time of Eustathius but was also strongly influenced by Eusebius of Caesarea and had spent some time at Alexandria completing his studies; Apollinaris was born and brought up in Laodicea under the influence of Antioch, but his father (also named Apollinaris), who was a teacher and doubtless saw to the education of his son, was from Alexandria and in theological matters the Alexandrian influence on our Apollinaris was decisive.

Despite their diverse cultural backgrounds, the three came to be close in their preference for the literal interpretation of Scripture, but without reaching radical positions. For Acacius and Apollinaris we have only fragments transmitted indirectly, and cannot say much. The title of Acacius' exegetical work in six books, *Selected Questions*, itself suggests interest in the more controversial and problematic aspects of the sacred text, a feature in keeping with the new tastes of the period, and this is confirmed by the subject-matter of various fragments which have reached us: the firmament and the form of the world (Gen. 1:6-8); the nourishment of incorporeal beings (Gen. 18:8); the apparent contradiction of certain Old Testament texts on the punishment of sin (pp. 110, 115, 118, Devreesse). As to Apollinaris, who was famous as an exegete in his own day, his former student Jerome passes a negative judgment: his exegesis was over-concise, his use of Greek translations of the Old Testament was confused (PL 24, 21f.; 23, 477). The extant fragments show a clear preference for literal interpretation, but with some concessions to moral application, and to traditional typology: in Gen. 49:27, Benjamin is the *typos* of Paul, according to a typology also found in Hippolytus; Num. 10:33, the advancing ark of the covenant, is a symbol of Christ who has gone before us to the place of rest (pp. 132, 139, Devreesse). The fragments on the Psalms offer much less frequent christological application than in Eusebius, but not as restricted as in Diodorus or Theodore of Mopsuestia.

The surviving fragments of Eusebius of Emesa on the books of the Law also show a clear, if not exclusive, propensity for literal interpretation (Joseph is a type of Christ: p. 79, Devreesse). The textual difficulties of the account of Abraham's journey of from the land of the Chaldeas to Canaan, are resolved without recourse to allegory by the Alexandrians. The extant fragments on Gen. 49, the blessings of Jacob, which since the 2nd century had been material for complete typological interpretation, all read the text in a literal manner (pp. 66, 81f., Devreesse).[12] But in the case of Eusebius of Emesa, we are more fortunate than with Acacius or Apollinaris, because a series of homilies preserved in Latin translation includes one of considerable exegetical significance: number 11, *De arbore fici* (Matt. 21:18-22). Here the author takes up a position on allegorical exegesis of Scripture: a balanced position: 'We do not reject all allegories, but neither do we merely accept them all' (p. 258, Buytaert). But, the balance is more apparent than real, because Eusebius goes on to notice that allegory charms the ears, surreptitiously complicates the sense of the text, and looks for easy escapes from real difficulties (pp. 258, 261). This is a criticism which we previously saw Porphyry level against Christians, and Origen in particular. And Eusebius scorns Origen's interpretation of just this passage especially where he rejects (p. 270) the allegory of the mountain representing Satan (Origen, *Comm. in Mt.* XVI 26).

Eusebius' interpretation of Matt. 21:18-22 is faithfully echoed by Ephrem (SC 121, 281ff.), proof of the influence of the new exegetical tendencies on this writer who was active between 330 and 370 in the inland, less Hellenised area of Syria (Nisibis, Edessa) and wrote in Syriac. In fact, even if he knows the traditional typological interpretation of the Old Testament (CSCO 152, 1f.), in his own systematic commentary on many episodes of Genesis and Exodus, he adheres almost exclusively to the literal interpretation of Scripture and only rarely mentions a christological *typos*: the ram of Gen. 22:13 is a symbol of Christ; Manasseh and Ephraim in Gen. 48:1ff., are symbols of Jews and Christians; Moses' staff which sweetens the bitter waters of Marah (Ex. 15:22f.) is a symbol of the cross (CSCO 152, 69, 93, 125). Only Gen. 49 (Blessings of the Patriarchs) is the object of a brief but systematic typological interpretation which follows a literal reading (94ff.): but while Hippolytus had based his interpretation on the juxtaposition: Judah/Reuben: Christians/Jews, Ephrem sees in Reuben the *typos* of Adam the sinner, and develops instead the Pauline juxtaposition of Adam/Christ. In more general terms, we might say that Ephrem seems to be detached from the scholarly, historical, or 'scientific' interests which were in evidence in other contemporary Syro-palestinian exegesis: the ingenuous and unsophisticated literalism used to interpret the early chapters of Genesis, while sometimes polemical towards Alexandrian allegorism (p. 5), is on the whole still connected with the Asiatic form of interpretation.

In relation to the New Testament, we have some commentaries by Ephrem on Paul, and one very extensive commentary on the *Diatessaron* of Tatian (a conflation of passages from the four Gospels to make a complete account of the life of Jesus without repetitions, written originally in Syriac and highly successful in antiquity). In this commentary there are certainly traces of allegory: the lost drachma in Lk. 15:8 is a symbol of Adam; Zacchaeus' climbing the fig tree (Lk. 19:4) symbolises his salvation (SC 121, 254, 278); but obviously the commentary is almost entirely literal. In opposition to the Gnostics, Ephrem likes to make frequent links between the Old and New Testaments: the healing of the woman with the haemorrhage is related to the episode in which Moses makes water gush from the rock; the tree which Zacchaeus climbs, recalls the tree of Adam's sin (pp. 152, 278). But above all, he loves to find in the Gospel text large openings for teaching and exhortation. The episode of the woman with the haemorrhage is interpreted on the basis of an association between touching Christ physically and touching him spiritually, which has an Origenistic flavour; Jesus walking on the water allows the interpreter to emphasise the reality of the human nature assumed by the Redeemer; the incident of the rich man and Lazarus inspires a comparison between the riches of heaven and those of earth (pp. 141, 217, 265).

3. *The Exegesis of the Cappadocians*

Cappadocia, which was always on the margin of the cultural life of the Church, has its moment of glory in the final decades of the 4th century with Basil, Gregory of Nazianzus and Gregory of Nyssa. In the preceding decades the area had shown itself as a breeding ground for Arianism, and here in passing we ought to mention Asterius the Sophist, a theorist of early Arianism whom Jerome (*De Viris Illustribus* 94) describes as the author of various exegetical works. About thirty homilies on the Psalms have been ascribed to him. Formally, very elaborate, with generous exhortatory development of a small number of biblical passages, and with frequent openings for a highly traditional christological typology: Joseph and David are figures of Christ; the symbolism of the vine (pp. 77f., 102, 105ff., Richard). Themes which are involved in the Arian controversy seem to be purposely avoided, suggesting that the author gradually distanced himself from active involvement in such polemics.

The exegetical activity of Basil was also exclusively homiletical, and a few homilies have come down to us. As is well known, Basil admired Origen, and the *Philokalia*, an anthology of excerpts from Origen's works, compiled by Basil together with Gregory of Nazianzus, has preserved for us the Greek text of the entire treatise on Scripture and the criteria for its interpretation in *De Princ.* IV 1-3). But the surviving homilies, a series on the *Hexaemeron*[13] and a few on the Psalms, devote very little attention to such criteria favouring a predominately literal exegesis, with obvious exhoratory and ethical objectives.

In the *Homilies on the Hexaemeron*, Basil does not shy away from displaying his stylistic virtuosity or his scientific competence: in fact, the biblical account of creation constituted the fundamental text which informed Christians about the world and nature, and Basil uses contemporary scientific knowledge to illustrate its terse account. Homilies 7, 8 and 9, which illustrate the biblical account of the creation of animals, amount to a review of the zoological knowledge of the time. Homilies 2 and 3 discuss problems relating to the nature of matter. In the first of the two (PG 29, 40) Basil expressly claims that he rejects an allegorical interpretation in order to adhere to the literal meaning of the text; and in Homily 3, discarding an allegorical interpretation which saw the waters above and below the firmament in Gen. 1:7 as symbols of angelic powers, he described it as a fantasy, or old men's tales (73f.). Given that the interpretation is actually that of Origen, the strong tone of the criticism is striking, but perhaps Basil had in his sights not so much the Alexandrian himself as one of his followers.

Literal interpretation with a view to edification and exhortation is predominant in the few extant homilies on the Psalms: only Ps. 44 is interpreted christologically; but not, for example, Ps. 1, which Eusebius following Origen, had referred to Christ, even if only in a general way. And yet, these homilies still show examples of exegetical procedures more typical of Alexandrian taste, such as having recourse to the etymology of Hebrew names (PG 29, 229). At the beginning of the homily on Ps. 1, Basil affirms that the Psalter epitomises all that is useful in the whole of Scripture (212): we have already touched on the same concept in Eusebius and we shall meet it again in Athanasius.

At this point we can also include the text: *On the Titles of the Psalms* by Gregory of Nyssa. On the basis of the titles which accompany the Psalms, he retains their traditional subdivision into five groups 1-40; 41-71; 72-88; 89-105; 106-150, and interprets them so as to present the progressive ascent of man from the moment when he turns away from sin, until the attainment of final beatitude, which consists in achieving the likeness of God. (PG 44, 433). In book II 2, Gregory offers a profession of allegorical faith: the historical events narrated in Scripture are not intended to increase our knowledge, but rather to educate us in the practice of virtue; to this end, the literal account refers us to a higher meaning. In fact, Gregory was above all a mystic and his interpretation of Scripture tends to uncover a mystical type of meaning. We could say that the whole of Gregory's later exegesis tends to develop the theme which we have found in his treatise *On the Titles of the Psalms*.

Gregory was not always like this. In his earliest sorties into exegesis, writing to defend and complete his brother's *Hexaemeron*, he warns against the confusion which allegorical interpretation of a text can provoke (PG 44, 81), and at the conclusion of the work he boasts of having explained the biblical text in a way which stays closest to the meaning of the actual words: and yet, for the waters of the firmament, he goes back to Origen's interpretation, so much criticised by Basil because he is convinced that this is not allegorical but literal (ibid.). The fact is that Gregory is too Origenistic, too spiritual, to be able to limit himself to a purely literal interpretation of Scripture, with the result that it is precisely allegorical interpretation, the type which we have labelled psychological or moral, that is for him the most congenial means of interpreting the sacred text.

We have already recorded the allegorical stamp of the work, *On the Titles of the Psalms*. At the beginning of his *Commentary on the Song of Songs*,[14] Gregory argues with all his strength against literalists: the criterion which ought to direct the interpretation of Scripture, is the usefulness which can be gained from it; sometimes the literal sense supplies this; at others the sacred text expresses itself enigmatically and in parables which require a more elevated interpretation: anagogy, tropology, allegory, call it what you will. The concept is illustrated by classic references to Gal. 4:21 and 2 Cor. 3:6, to which are added various prophetic texts. In fact, the Song of Songs was the text which most encouraged allegory, and Gregory, referring back to Origen, takes up and develops themes relating to the love of the soul for the Logos and its ascent to the Logos.

Among the other exegetical works of Gregory, *The Life of Moses* above all deserves mention. Even though the basic theme may be the same as that illustrated above, the soul's ascent to God, the treatment is conducted with greater regard for the letter of the texts of Exodus and Numbers, which describe the life of Moses. The book is divided into two parts. The first presents the events of Moses historically (Gregory aptly calls this *historia*): the second (*theoria*) interprets the same texts allegorically, following the theme of the mind's journey to God. Before becoming a theme of Origen's, this had been taken up by Philo in his exegesis of Exodus and Numbers, and Philo's influence remains strong in Gregory's work; consider only the interpretation of the darkness which surrounds Moses as he climbs the mountain, symbolising the transcendence of divine nature (SC 1 *bis,* 80ff.). But, thanks to traditional typology, Gregory can filter Philo's influence into a more exact historical dimension, as Clement and Origen had already done: the crossing of the Red Sea is a *typos* of baptism; the twelve springs and seventy palm trees of Ex. 15:27 are symbols of the apostles and the disciples of Christ; the manna which changed according to the spiritual conditions of those who gathered it is a symbol of the Logos who accommodates the spiritual dispositions of those who receive him, by virtue of the diversity of his qualities, a typically Origenistic theme (pp. 67f., 70f., 73).

4. *Antiochene Exegesis*

Coming, after this Cappadocian interlude, to the Antiochene school proper, we should clarify at once that the word *school* in this context should not suggest an actual *didaskaleion,* like that of Alexandria, i.e. a scholastic institution, properly organised and placed under the patronage and supervision of the local bishop. At Antioch, we have instead a group of exegetes and theologians, some of whom, like Diodorus, also had a private and personal teaching role. The group was closely united within itself, less by student-teacher relationships than by a common stamp of theology and exegesis.

With regard to exegesis, which is our sole present concern, scholars had long contrasted this school with that of Alexandria, as promoting a literal style of exegesis. But recent decades have seen a tendency to reconsider the opposition between the two schools, recalling some non-literalist approaches in the Antiochene writers.[15] In fact, Diodorus juxtaposes allegory and *theoria,* so that, for him, while allegory weakens and abuses the letter of the text, *theoria* recognises a higher level of meaning which overlies the literal, without deleting or weakening it. Diodorus does not recognise demons in the abyss which Scripture mentions, or the devil in the serpent; but he does accept that the story of Cain and Abel, at a higher level of meaning, signifies the hostility of the Jews towards the Church (CCG 6, 7f.). This and other similar claims by Diodorus and Theodore show that Antiochene exegesis was not exclusively literalist, and tends to diminish the contrast between the Alexandrian and Antiochene Schools.

Having safely established the status of generalising outlines, it remains to be seen how they were put into practice, especially since, within their common exegetical outlook, the principal representatives of the Antiochine school – Diodorus, Theodore, John, Theodoret – do not give any impression of a monolithic block. Hence the necessity to study them individually.[16]

We can start with Diodorus, the actual founder of the School, who was active in the final decades of the 4th century, and whose important distinction between allegory and *theoria* has already been mentioned. All the surviving texts present him as strongly literalist: in Gen. 49, the blessings of Jacob, only vv. 10-12, relating to the patriarch Judah and already understood as messianic by the Jews are taken as a prophecy of Christ. The traditional typological reading is rejected for the remainder of the passage (pp. 128ff., De Coninck). Within the group of Psalms 1-50,[17] a christological interpretation is given only to Pss. 2, 8 and 44, once again only those previously interpreted as messianic by the Jews. Diodorus, who takes David to be the author of the Psalter, considers many psalms as prophecies of subsequent events, but referring almost exclusively to events in Jewish history (Maccabees, Hezekiah).[18] It does not seem that in this group of psalms, there was ever any question of superimposing a higher meaning on the literal sense: Pss. 2, 8 and 44 are exclusively christological, the others are simply historical, referring to various events in the history of Israel. A particular characteristic of the exegesis of Diodorus is the internal coherence of his interpretation of any single context: Gen. 49 is interpreted on the principle that the words of Jacob spoken to his sons, the twelve patriarchs, are to be referred to the history, not of the patriarchs, but rather of the tribes which were named after them. This criterion is applied most strictly to the entire passage (pp. 128ff., De Coninck). Each psalm is preceded by an introduction which summarises its significance and characteristics, and the whole psalm is then interpreted in harmony with this: for Ps. 9, he denies that the term 'son' can be applied to Christ, because other details of this text cannot be fitted into such an interpretation (CCG 6, 51).

* * *

We know less about Diodorus than about his pupil Theodore of Mopsuestia, whose *Commentary on the Twelve Minor Prophets* survives in its entirety in its original Greek.[19] In *Commentary on Zechariah* 9:8-10 (PG 66, 556), Theodore spars with some who refer this context partly to Zerubbabel and partly to Christ, and claims that the Law contains a shadow of all the events of Christ (Heb. 10:1): in this way, certain statements of Scripture which seem heavily hyperbolic (*hyperbolikoteron*) when referred to individuals in the Old Testament are in fact totally fulfilled in Christ.[20] In the preface to *Commentary on Jonah* (320f.) Theodore treats events in the Old Testament as *typoi* of events in the New Testament; interprets the liberation of the Jews from Egypt as a prefiguration of the death of Christ and liberation from sin, and explains that the events of the Old Testament are *typoi* of those in the New Testament if they have some similarity with them, if they are useful in their own time, and if they are inferior to the future realities of which they are *typoi*. In this sense, Jonah is a perfect *typos* of Christ.

Thus, Theodore has a clear idea of the typological interpretation of the Old Testament. Yet, if we move from the statement of the theory to see how and where it is applied in his Commentary, we discover that at no point is Jonah described as a *typos* of Christ, and only six texts in all twelve of the Minor Prophets are given a christological sense: e.g. Joel 2:28-32, because quoted *ad litteram* in Acts 2:17-21 in relation to the outpouring of the Holy Spirit at Pentecost. Among the passages in the Twelve for which Theodore does not accept a christological interpretation, there are some which were famously taken in this way: Zech. 3:8 'I now mean to raise my servant . . .'; [Theodore, *sic*] and Mal. 4:2 (3:20 in the Septuagint): 'But for you . . . the sun of righteousness will rise.' Only occasionally does Theodore explain the reason for his refusal: on Micah 4:1-3 he observes that Micah 4:2 'For out of Zion shall go forth the law, and the word of the Lord from

Jerusalem' is contradictory to John 4:21 where Jesus says to the Samaritan woman that the time would come when the Father would no longer be worshipped in Jerusalem (364f.).

If we move from the Minor Prophets to the other texts of the Old Testament, we find that Theodore accepts a christological interpretation only for Pss. 2, 8, 44, and 109, i.e. those already accepted as messianic by the Jews;[21] as a general rule, he accepts the christological interpretation of a text only if it is applied to Christ in the New Testament in the most explicit way; he cannot be satisfied with a mere allusion.[22] We might add that he alone among early exegetes does not accept the traditional interpretation of the couple in the Song of Songs as Christ and the Church, and reads the work as a simple love song, for which reason he rejects its full canonicity. It is indisputable that Theodore has reduced the presence of Christ in the Old Testament to the barest necessary minimum. He tends, like his Jewish contemporaries, to see prophecies, which Christians and often earlier Jews had taken to be messianic, as having been fulfilled in the post-exilic period of Israel's history (Zerubbabel, Maccabees),[23] and thus he viewed the Old Testament dispensation as complete in itself, with very few direct links with the dispensation of the New.

Theodore was driven to emphasise the gap between the Old Testament and the New more than the continuity. This resulted not only by a literalist style of scriptural interpretation, but also by doctrinal considerations. He places Christianity third in human history, after paganism and Judaism: completely opposed to the first, and complementary to the second, in that it brought the knowledge of the mystery of divine birth and the incarnation.Thus the knowledge of God has passed through three stages: polytheism, monotheism, and trinitarianism (*Comm. in Jo.* 17:3; CSCO 116, 221). Then reviewing the entire present era as a whole, this life of a world dominated by sin and misery, he contrasts it with the future era, which will be characterised by the absence of sin, and consequently, will be a state of perfection and happiness.[24] But in the course of the present era, the incarnation of the Logos has started a new direction in the history of the world, representing the anticipation of the era to come, and contrasting the former domination by the Law with the new dispensation of the spirit and of grace. It is entirely directed towards the moment of the final consummation, of which it is the foretaste and the promise. Theodore, who makes little use of *typos* to underline the connection of the Old and New Testaments, instead makes great use of that term to indicate the relationship between the baptism of the individual Christian and the baptism of Christ. Baptismal regeneration may be understood as a *typos* of the true, eternal birth which will occur in the resurrection of the dead. In short, Theodore prefers to locate the relationship of anticipation and prefiguration which the allegorists established between the Old and New Testaments, between Christian initiation and its fulfilment in the era to come. The clearly eschatological thrust of this idea found little significance in Old Testament/New Testament continuity, i.e. in the presence of Christ in the Old Testament revealed by typological, allegorical, interpretation of the Old Testament text. The few, albeit convinced concessions which he makes to christological interpretation of the Old Testament (*typoi* and prophecies) do not alter the fundamental thrust of Theodore's conception of hermeneutics, which pointed him in the literalist direction.

This literalism in harmony with the tastes of the period, translated itself into an interest in the history of Israel. As far as we can gather from surviving material, Theodore prefaces his commentary on each of the minor prophets, and and even on individual psalms, with an introduction fixing its historical setting, and general features precisely, and he develops his commentary entirely in line with these programmatic prefaces. The commentary flows swiftly, packed with historical references and alert to grammatical and linguistic features of the text, all with the aim of setting out accurately its literal meaning. The tendency towards conciseness is such that, on occasion, parts of his commentaries are nothing more than paraphrases of the scriptural text itself. A sufficient example would be the commentary on Zech. 10 (PG 66, 564ff.).

In the introduction to his commentary on John (CSCO 116, 2), Theodore observes that the business of exegesis is to explain difficult expressions in the biblical text, without superfluous digressions, which are permitted, even required of the preacher. He is obviously alluding to the verbose commentaries of the Alexandrian exegetes, and the contrast between the conciseness of Antiochene commentaries[25] and the prolixity of the Alexandrians (Origen, Didymus) does indeed highlight their divergent approach to Scripture. The Antiochene perceives in the sacred text a precise meaning to be illustrated without frills in a reading which adheres to the literal sense. The Alexandrian sees it as pregnant with meaning and with depth of mystery, to be read at several levels, and needing patient excavation to uncover, at least partly, its richness of meaning.

Theodore devotes unusual attention to pointing out passages in which the sacred text makes use of either numbers or figurative language. Opposing the allegorists, he never tires of declaring that numbers merely indicate a particular quantity and have no symbolic value. Only by remembering this polemical attitude can one understand why he goes into such otherwise seemingly banal details as the three and four transgressions of Damascus (*Comm. in Amos* 1:3-5; PG 66, 249); the ten men mentioned in *Comm. in Zech.* 8:23 (552); the three shepherds in the *Comm. in Zech.* 11:7-8 (573).

His particular attention to the use of figurative language is equally anti-allegorical. Allegorists habitually used such figurative expressions, which they would take in a rigidly literal and thus arbitrary manner, to produce an allegorical meaning from the apparent incongruency of the passage. Theodore, by contrast, correctly emphasises the figurative quality of the language, which can even become symbolic, as being integral to the first, literal meaning of the text. In his commentary on the vision in Zech. 1:18-21, Theodore repudiates the interpretation of those who perceive in the four horns a symbol of the Assyrians, the Babylonians, the Medes and the Persians, and takes them more simply, though still symbolically, as a reference to the four cardinal points of the compass (PG 66, 513f.). Ashkelon in Zeph. 2:7 by synecdoche (part for the whole) stands for all the foreign cities of the Palestinian coast (461); the expression: 'His dominion shall be from sea to sea,.....' in Zech. 9:10-12, said of Zerubbabel, indicates by hyperbole the victories and conquests of the Israelite leader

(561). Theodore takes pains to point out such hyperboles, since their exaggerations were particularly liable to encourage the use of allegorical procedures.

Being the literalist that he is, Theodore very occasionally bow to traditional usage by accepting a typological interpretation of the Old Testament; when it comes to the New Testament, he is absolutely literalist. Commenting on Gal. 4:24, where Paul says that the statement that Abraham had two sons was made allegorically, Theodore accuses the allegorists of abusing Paul's expression to eliminate the actual scriptural meaning, and to invent foolish fables. For them, Adam is not Adam, paradise is not paradise, the serpent is not the serpent. In fact, Paul had no intention of suppressing the historicity of Abraham's two sons, but rather intended to make use of the expression for his own purposes. In this case, Theodore's is a minimalist interpretation of Paul's text, in that Paul is taken to have established, between Abraham's two sons on the one hand and the two Testaments on the other, a relationship of similarity and comparison (pp. 73ff., Swete), i.e. a purely external connection. While the relationship actually intended by Paul was undoubtedly a stronger and more significant one of symbolic anticipation.

The Gospel of John, given its more sustained doctrinal tone in comparison to the other gospels, normally prompted the early exegetes to an interpretation in which the doctrinal element is strong: this is also true of Theodore's commentary. Engaged in the christological debate on the anti-Apollinarian side, even if he is often preoccupied with demonstrating the union, in Christ, of the human and divine nature in a single *prosopon*, on the whole, he shows clearly the limitations of his christology, which does not really manage to unite in a satisfactory way the two subjects, human and divine, which he sees in operation in Christ. More generally, his rigidly literal exegesis ignores the fact that various details of the Fourth Gospel obviously have a symbolic value, and in these instances, he is unsatisfactory. The fact that John twice specifies that it was by the well of Jacob that the conversation between Jesus and the Samaritan woman unfolds (4:5,12), has no significance for Theodore. The fact that the official's son was cured at the seventh hour (4:52) is for him merely a chronological detail (CSCO 116, 61f., 69). Theodore is undoubtedly more at ease in his interpretation of Paul, given the tendency outlined above to separate quite distinctly the old and new dispensations. His introductory remarks to the various letters are a model of information and the major themes of Paul's message (the relationship between Jews and Christians, justification and freedom) are explored with complete faithfulness to Paul's thought.

* * *

John Chrysostom was, from a literary point of view, the most prominent personality among the Antiochenes for the effectiveness and the power of his oratory, which shows itself particularly in the systematic explanation of many books of both the Old and New Testament. He is of less interest to us from the specifically exegetical standpoint, since the primary objective of his rhetorical output was to draw out of the sacred text a lesson to educate, warn, or edify his listeners, rather than to illustrate the text for its own sake. It will be enough to note that the myriad possibilities which John could find in the text which had just been read to his congregation are based on a rigorously literal reading of it, something which shows his full adherence to Antiochene exegetical precepts. His predominately ethical or exhortatory interest accounts for the fact that often the actual illustration of the text remains superficial. It is symptomatic that his homilies on Matthew are, on the whole, much more expansive than those on John, because the First Gospel is particularly suited to moral teaching, while the Fourth invites a more theological explanation which, a few specific cases apart, holds less interest for John. The illustration of the letters of Paul is similarly deficient.

Theodoret, who was active a few decades after Theodore and John Chrysostom and wrote several specifically exegetical works, interests us especially because, while clearly of an Antiochene persuasion, he takes pains to moderate the rigid literalism of Diodorus and Theodore, making room for the traditional christological interpretation of the Old Testament.

For example, Isaac's blessing of Jacob (Gen. 27:27ff.) is applied to the incarnation of Christ, Jacob's blessing of Dan (Gen. 49:17) is applied to the Antichrist, Moses' Ethiopian wife becomes the *typos* of pagans who convert to the Church; Moses' prayer with uplifted hands in Ex. 17:11 is symbolic of the redeeming power of the incarnation (PG 80, 189, 221, 228, 261). In his interpretation of the Minor Prophets, Theodoret sometimes takes up the traditional christological interpretations which Theodore had rejected, e.g. chap. 14 of Zechariah and Mal. 4:2 (the sun of righteousness) (PG 81, 1952ff.). It is worth emphasising that this retrieval of christological references after Theodore's reluctance, should be understood solely as the mitigation of a literalism whose intransigence took no account of ancient and established exegetical traditions. It does not imply any general re-examination of the relationship between literal and typological interpretations of the Old Testament.[26] In the introduction to his *Commentary on the Psalms,* Theodoret restricts himself to noting that David on occasion also prophesied the incarnation, passion and resurrection of Christ (PG 80, 861).

The *Commentary on the Song of Songs* represents the high point of Theodoret's divergence from Theodore and thus likewise the greatest *rapprochement* to Alexandrian hermeneutics. Without naming him specifically, his intention is to react against Theodore's claim that the Song of Songs was purely a profane love song (PG 81, 29) and he recognises its traditional christological and ecclesial significance. Given too the clearly homogeneous character of the love-song of the bride and groom, it must surely be interpreted in a similarly homogeneous manner, i.e. in a completely allegorical sense. To justify this departure from the usual hermeneutical norms of Antiochene circles, he demonstrates in the introduction to his commentary that the symbolic character of certain prophetic passages is beyond doubt: the eagle of Ezek. 17:3-4 is a symbol of Nebuchadnezzar who destroys Jerusalem (33f.). The interpretation strictly follows that of Origen, sometimes in detail and he also takes from him allegories based on etymologies of Hebrew names: Engedi = temptation, Bethel = the house of God (84, 100); there is also the usual terminology.

It is remarkable to read in an Antiochene text references to allegory and to its laws, and a rebuke to those who would refuse to go beyond the veil of the letter, and who interpret the text in a fleshly sense without penetrating to its spirit (32–33, 40). Origen, as we have noted, gave a threefold interpretation of every part of the Song of Songs: one literal and two spiritual; Theodoret gives only one, the spiritual. But precisely at this level, where he seems most in line with Origen, Theodroet shows that his closeness to Alexandrian hermeneutics is occasional and superficial. Such hermeneutics had been based on the distinction of several levels of interpretation (usually two or three); Theodoret limits himself to one only, which in this very special case cannot be the literal one, but must be the spiritual. The brevity of Theodoret's commentary which ruthlessly prune's Origen's full treatment, is once again, in its external approach, a tell-tale sign of how fundamentally foreign to the Antiochene are the interpretative methods adopted *en bloc* from Alexandria.

In the introduction to his commentary on Paul (PG 82, 37), Theodoret justifies his habitual brevity by the need to accommodate the sluggish reader. Perhaps this is symptomatic of a certain weariness among the Christian community for exegetical works of large dimensions – a foretaste of that demand for anthologies and easily readable manuals which is characteristic of literary and cultural decline in general. This background also helps to explain the form of a compact group of exegetical works by Theodoret, dealing with almost all the books of the Law and the historical books, which explain points that raise difficulties of interpretation, in question and answer form, a form which was to prove very successful also in the West. We might add that more once, Theodoret claims to present in his works the fruit of the labour of earlier exegetes (PG 81, 48, 1257, 1548). Such claims should be viewed in a relative manner, because Theodoret himself is well able to interpret a text, but there is no doubt that he used the writings of others, which he sometimes even quotes in full to give the reader a wider exegetical perspective (cf., for example, PG 80, 108ff. with quotations from Diodorus, Theodore and Origen).

All these are signs of weariness which herald the end of the heyday of Antiochene exegesis. In fact, the christological controversies of the 5th century which had their epicentre in Antioch, radically transformed the contextual setting which had been instrumental in developing the doctrinal and exegetical character of the Antiochene School and weakened its vitality. But the coherence of its exegetical literalism had by now set up a valid alternative to Alexandrian allegory, and its effects were felt immediately, even in the West.

5. *Alexandrian Exgesis*

In the preceding pages we have seen how the tendency to modify the use of allegorical interpretation had extended, in the course of the 4th century, well beyond specifically Antiochene territory,[27] even into areas such as Palestine, which had been strongly influenced by Alexandria. But, it does not seem that such a tendency had any appreciable impact on specifically Alexandrian exegesis in the course of that century.[28] Athanasius only holds marginal interest for us, because he himself took little interest in exegesis. We might, however, recall his letter to Marcellinus on the interpretation of the Psalms as further evidence of an earlier conviction that the Psalter contained in concentrated form, all that was of value in the other Old Testament books (chap. 2). The Psalter by now had become a book of personal devotion for the Christian, and Athanasius carefully divides the Psalms into various groups, according to subject and literary form, in such a way that the devout reader could choose among them according to circumstances (14ff.). Christological Psalms are given a very considerable place in this collection: apart from specifically recommending many, Athanasius adds that christological references can be found in almost all of them (26). We are far removed from the restrictive criteria which were becoming current in Antiochene circles.

Specifically exegetical activity predominates, however in Didymus the Blind, the last great exponent of the Alexandrian School,[29] active in the second half of the 4th century.[30] We will not dwell on him very long, because he was a particularly faithful disciple of Origen, and his every page, though less suggestive and brilliant than the master's, reflects his interpretative method almost slavishly. Like Origen, Didymus is convinced that both Old and New Testament, under their obscurity, conceal supernatural mysteries; the literal sense (*historia*) can be a step towards uncovering these, but only the anagogical sense can arrive at them through allegory.[31] Thus Didymus, like Origen, reads Scripture at two different levels, and to pass from one to the other he uses all the procedures typical of Alexandrian exegesis: the deficiency of the literal sense, etymologies of Jewish names, symbolic value of numbers and of other entities, animals, plants, metals, parts of the body, and so on. Against this background, occasional reminders not to be excessive in allegorical interpretation (SC 233, 246) reveal at the level of theory, an anxiety not to offer a target to literalist criticisms, but they do not seem to have had much impact on the exegetical practice of our author.

Compared with Origen, Didymus is less interested in textual criticism, and references to other Greek translations to complement the Septuagint are less frequent. His interest in the 'psychological' style of exegesis sometimes leads to Philo's influence accompanying Origen's.

The *Commentary on Genesis*[32] merits a separate if brief mention. This is the oldest commentary by a Greek Christian author on this text which has come down to us in its entirety,[33] and it allows us to reconstruct certain interpretations from the lost commentary of the same name by Origen. The first three chapters of Genesis constituted the foundation of Christian anthropology, and the debate between Asiatics, who read the story of the creation and fall literally, and Alexandrians who allegorised it extensively, was particularly sharp over these chapters. Despite contemporary criticisms of Origen's interpretation in this area, Didymus follows him faithfully. He not only distinguishes like all Alexandrians (Philo, Clement, Origen) between man in the image of God (Gen. 1:26) i.e. the soul or the inner man, and man moulded formed of dust from the ground (Gen. 2:7); but like Origen he distinguishes between the lighter, spiritual body before the fall, and the heavy, dense body with which Adam and Eve were clothed after the fall (=the clothes made out of skins in Gen. 3:21) (SC 233, 156ff., 250ff., 276).

The combination of the influence of Philo with that of Origen is particularly evident in the interpretation of Gen. 16:1-2 (Hagar and Sarah), where Didymus, after briefly recalling the Pauline interpretation in Gal. 4:21ff. (Hagar and Sarah are *typoi* of the two testaments), goes on to introduce the name of Philo as the author of an interpretation which saw Sarah as the symbol of perfect virtue, and Hagar as the symbol of the preliminary exercises leading to such virtue (SC 244, 202f.). The total adherence of Didymus to the interpretative methods of the Alexandrian tradition is further displayed in a theoretical aside prefaced to his interpretation of Gen. 6:13: many passages of Scripture, even when only read literally, are profitable for the many, who live by sensation and opinion alone; even a literal interpretation of the miracles of Jesus can be useful (the raising of Lazarus, the curing of the man born blind, etc.). But they also have a symbolic value: the spiritual healing of the soul, which is more important than the literal sense, but ignored by the majority. It would be superfluous to underline the parallel between this passage (SC 244, 62f.) and the correlation established by Origen: the unsophisticated (= the many) – the literal sense of Scripture / the perfect (=few) – the spiritual sense.

At first glance, the exegesis of *Cyril* also remains faithful to the Alexandrian methods. The *Glaphyra* on the five books of the Pentateuch are a series of passages chosen for interpretation, with a quite Alexandrian prolixity, in a christological sense, from Cain and Abel, figures respectively of the Jews and of Christ, down to Joshua, also a figure of Christ. The prophecies of the book of Isaiah are read christologically, using specifically allegorical procedures: the Lebanon of Is. 10:34 is a symbol of the Temple in Jerusalem; Idumea in Is. 24:5 is a symbol of the Church; the islands of Is. 41:1 are a symbol of pagans who convert to Christ (PG 70, 308, 741, 825). His *Commentary on the Twelve Minor Prophets*, gives, with much Alexandrian terminology in which the spiritual sense is the authentic one, as opposed to any crude literal interpretation (PG 71, 49, 577, 580), an interpretation in contrast to that of Theodore in the enormous space it accords to the christological interpretation which he had neglected. Here Cyril also takes up Origen's distinction between the spiritual sense (i.e. the christological sense strictly speaking) and the moral sense (i.e. the application of the prophetic text to the daily life of the Christian), e.g. in the Commentary on Joel 1:11-12 (PG 71, 345) the calamities which afflict the fields of Israel are first interpreted literally, then referred spiritually to the punishment which the Jews underwent at the hands of the Romans for their rejection of Christ, and finally, are referred morally to the condition of the soul, a garden which flourishes with virtues, but withers with vice. It might be noted here that sometimes the christological reading of the prophetic text is superimposed on the literal reading, as a higher level; and sometimes constitutes the only reading of the text, e.g. the destruction of the vine and the fig in Hosea 2:12; this indicates literally the wretchedness of Israel fallen prey to invaders, and spiritually the diminishing importance of the Law, which the Jews failed to use as a schoolmaster leading to Christ; but the continuation of the text, from verse 14b onwards, is taken in a christological sense only, in as much as: 'In these words the passage manifestly (i.e. in a direct and immediate way) promises us salvation through Christ' (PG 71, 76f., 81ff.). It would be superfluous to add that Cyril makes wide use of hermeneutical procedures which by now we recognise as typically Alexandrian, even if he shows greater reserve in number symbolism than Didymus who had a special predilection for this symbolism.[34]

A more attentive study of Cyril's commentary reveals two characteristics which are closely linked: the literal interpretation is highly developed, much more so than in any other Alexandrian exegete; the spiritual level is frequently missing altogether, and in these cases the literal interpretation is either accompanied only by the moral interpretation or it is on its own. Even in the *Commentary on Isaiah*, many passages are interpreted only in a literal fashion, in reference to the Ayssrian invasions of Palestine; and even in the *Glaphyra*, where the spiritual interpretation is systematic, the literal reading which precedes it for each passage is extensive. In substance, we see a moderation by Cyril of the basic axiom which underlies the exegesis of Origen and Didymus, viz. that all of Scripture has a spiritual meaning.

Cyril, in the introduction to his *Commentary on Jonah* (PG 71, 600f.), illustrates this hermeneutical praxis. He retains the traditional typology of Jonah as a *typos* of Christ, but he adds a fundamental restraint on this, which he demonstrates by using the example of Moses. Even if Moses was a *typos* of Christ, not everything that Scripture says of Moses can be referred to Christ:[35] 'Thus not all that is expressed in the letter and in the *typoi* is helpful for spiritual interpretation, but if an individual is presented whose person figures Christ, we will disregard mere human connotations and linger instead only on what is necessary, gathering together from everywhere what might be useful for the purpose in hand' (PG 71, 601). Jonah is a figure of Christ in the three days which he spent in the belly of the fish, but not when he tried to escape God's command or when he grieved over the pardon granted by God to Nineveh.

Thus for Cyril not all of the Old Testament should be read in a christological sense, but only certain passages: the *Glaphyra* are an obvious application of this criterion, in that Cyril has here selected from the vast material at his disposal in the Pentateuch, only a few texts for which a typological (i.e. christological) interpretation was not only traditional, but easily recoverable at the level of the letter of the text.

As to Cyril's reasons for abandoning the exegetical criterion of Origen, we can observe generally that Cyril, in the middle of the Origenist controversy, would certainly feel less bound to Origen's legacy than Didymus. Detachment from it would have been encouraged also by Cyril's obvious interest in the history of Israel, in keeping with the tastes of his day, which on this point take him further even than Theodore. The preface to his commentary on Hosea, the first of the Minor Prophets, contains a lengthy treatment of Solomon and the division of the kingdom of Israel; the commentary on the very short Book of Obadiah contains a long excursus on the Edomites, and so we could go on. But it is obvious that this partial abandonment of Alexandrian hermeneutical methods was principally motivated by the need to find a plausible line of defence against the anti-allegorical offensive of the Antiochenes, which preoccupied

Didymus as we have seen, more in theory than in practice. Before the accusation of allegorising the whole of Scripture in a forced and arbitrary manner, Cyril decided to occupy a more moderate position, particularly because the deeper philosophical and spiritual motives which provided the ideological basis for Origen's hermeneutics were foreign to him. Cyril's Old Testament exegesis, the product of conflicting tensions, maintained a middle position, unable or unwilling to reject *in toto* traditional Alexandrian criteria in favour of those of Antioch. Consequently, it lost, with the more radical aspects, the wholeness and compactness typical of the best Alexandrian tradition.[36]

In his interpreting of the New Testament, it was even more difficult to sustain the allegorising thrust of Origen: both in his *Commentary on John* and in his homilies on Luke, Cyril interprets the activity of Jesus in a predominately literal manner. The primary interest of the Commentary is, however, doctrinal, given the particular character of the Fourth Gospel; more specifically, it is anti-Arian. The homilies on Luke, either because of the homiletical form or because of the nature of the Third Gospel, have a more practical scope. Here, introducing the interpretation of the difficult parable of the dishonest steward (Lk. 16:1ff.), Cyril makes the observation that parables should not be given too meticulous or subtle an interpretation since this makes for obscure prolixity; and only certain parts of them should be interpreted allegorically, to extract what may help the listeners (PG 72, 809f.). A little earlier, he had interpreted the parable of the prodigal son, rejecting various complicated interpretations and referring it simply to divine mercy towards sinners. Yet, Cyril is anything but systematically faithful to this criterion of the simple reading of the text. In fact, not only is subtle interpretation of detail found in other parables (e.g. the two denarii in the parable of the Good Samaritan represent the two Testaments (681)), but an allegorical interpretation is accorded even to details of the narrative text which can perfectly be understood in a literal way. In the eschatological discourse (Lk. 17:20ff.), those who are on the rooftops are a symbol of people of high standing; those who are in bed symbolise those who live for pleasure;

Zacchaeus, who sees Christ from the top of the sycamore tree (Lk. 19:4), symbolises those who come to Christ raising themselves above the passions of the world (844, 845, 865).

In the Commentary on John, too, there is no lack of very complex allegories: the five barley loaves in the miracle of the multiplication of the loaves (Jn. 6:9), are the five books of the Law which give poor nourishment if taken literally; the two fish, more gratifying food, represent evangelical and apostolic preaching (PG 73, 456). On the whole we can say that the way in which Cyril's interpretation of the Gospels passes from the literal to the allegorical level, displays something desultory and casual, which confirms the impression of the lack of wholeness and compactness already witnessed in his Old Testament exegesis.

NOTES

[1.] This last characteristic is to be seen much more in the exegesis of the East than of the West.

[2.] On this point cf. J. Pépin, *Mythe et allégorie*, Paris 1958, p. 132ff.

[3.] These refer to the appearances of God to the patriarchs and to Moses. Following a tradition going back to the 2nd century, Eusebius takes the Logos, the Son of God, as the object of these, rather than God the Father.

[4.] In the literal sense the reference to Egypt can indicate the journey into Egypt of Jesus, Mary and Joseph (Matt. 2:13ff.). Eusebius specifies at the end of the chapter that all the rest of the prophecy is to be interpreted allegorically. In IV 11 Egypt again allegorically represents human life.

[5.] The text of this commentary in PG 24, taken from Catenae, is fairly unreliable. The 1975 edition of J. Ziegler in GCS, *Eusebius' Werke IX*, should be used.

[6.] That is, so that the interpretation goes beyond the first sense of the prophetic text.

[7.] Sometimes the christological sense is superimposed on another more obvious one: Is. 45:2 is historically referred to Cyrus and Zerubbabel and spiritually to Christ.

[8.] Eusebius uses typically Alexandrian methods for the exegesis of details (symbolism of numbers, etymology of Hebrew names), but less frequently than Origen.

[9.] The text of the Commentary as it we have it is reliable only for Pss. 51-100; for the preceding Psalms, the extant fragments are many and often reliable; for the following, they are few and uncertain.

[10.] Cf., for example, the commentary on Ps. 51 and Ps. 53.

[11.] The term should be understood in the usual cultural sense rather than in the strict geographical sense.

[12.] Jerome also underlines the historical, i.e. literal, nature of the exegesis of Eusebius of Emesa.

[13.]The name indicates the account in Genesis of the creation of the world in six days.

[14.]This commentary like others of Gregory (on Ecclesiastes, on the Lord's Prayer), seems to come from collections of sermons.

[15.]This about-turn was determined by A. Vaccai, 'La teoria esegetica antiochena', *Biblica* 15 (1934), 94-101.

[16.]We will stay mostly with Theodore of Mopsuestia, the most important representative of the school. Much less material has come down to us from the leader of the school Diodorus, who was also the author of *On the Difference Between Theoria and* Allegoria.

[17.]Only for these psalms is the text currently available in CCG 6. This is the first part of a complete commentary, whose contested Diodoran authorship is well confirmed by the recent editor Olivier.

[18.]One should bear in mind the fact that the early exegetes soon noticed that many psalms made reference to events in the history of Israel much later than the time of David, down to the Exile and the Return from Exile. They reconciled this observation with the Jewish tradition of David's authorship of the Psalms by seeing such references as prophecies made by David.

[19.]We have Commentaries on the Fourth Gospel and on certain letters of Paul in Syriac and Latin respectively. To these are added many fragments and a partial Latin translation of the commentary on the Psalms by Julian of Eclanum. Theodore, along with many scriptural commentaries also wrote a theoretical work *Against Allegorists*.

[20.]This is substantially the Antiochene application of the old principle which based allegory upon the actual or presumed deficiency of the literal sense of the biblical text. For Diodorus' application of this to Ps. 22, cf. CCG 6, 268.

[21.]Theodore, like Diodorus before him, interprets these psalms in a christological sense only, without superimposing this on any historico-literal interpretation.

[22.]Cf. R. Devreesse, *Essai sur Théodore de Mopsueste*, Vatican City, 1948, p. 73ff.

[23.]In this sense, Pss. 59, 68, 79, which, as we saw, Eusebius considered christological, are applied by Theodore to the activities of the Maccabees.

[24.]On this point, see my 'Note sull'esegesi veterotestamentaria di Teodoro di Mopsuestia,' *Vetera Christianorum* 14 (1977), 84ff.

[25.]Not only those of Diodorus and Theodore, but also those of Theodoret and of John Chrysostom, taking from the latter only the strictly exegetical part.

[26.]In his New Testament exegesis, Theodoret is strictly literalist.

[27.]According to Jerome (*De Viris Illustribus*, 90), Theodore of Heraclia in Thrace, had a particularly literalist approach in his lost commentaries on the Psalms and on various books of the New Testament.

[28.]Cf., for a supposed Alexandrian opposition to Origen's exegesis, chapter 2, note 13 above.

[29.]That is, of the School in the strict sense, of which Didymus was the head, because Cyril should be taken as the last important representative of Alexandrian exegesis in general.

[30.]Various papyrus codices discovered at Tura in 1941 made known to us several commentaries on books of the Old Testament: Genesis, Psalms, Ecclesiastes, Job, Zechariah.

[31.]The term *anagoge* is frequently used by Didymus, more than 'allegory'. The relationship between the two terms is far from clear: *allegory* seems to indicate the interpretative procedure in a broad sense, while *anagoge* indicates the Christian content of the allegory. However, the two do seem fairly interchangeable.

[32.]The commentary extends from chap. 1 to chap. 16.

[33.]The papyrus, however, is in poor condition near the beginning and some parts are missing.

[34.]Cyril sparingly uses other Greek translations apart from the Septuagint, and he also makes reference to the Hebrew text.

[35.]Moses, Cyril observes, was not a skilful speaker, something which could not be said of Christ. Aaron, another *typos* of Christ, cannot be such when he slanders Moses.

[36.]We encounter a more completely Alexandrian observance in the *Commentary on Leviticus* by Hesychius of Jerusalem (first half of the 5th century), who interprets the Jewish legal prescriptions spiritually, applying them to the life of the Church and of the Christian.

Chapter 4

Exegetical Activity in the West

1. An Overview

The backwardness of Western Christian literature and culture compared to the East – a result of later evangelisation – is seen also in the study of Scripture. However, towards the end of the 2nd century in Africa, at least a partial translation had been made of the Greek text of the New Testament, and not long after, the whole Bible was available in the West in a Latin translation which followed the Greek text (for the Old Testament, the Septuagint) faithfully, even to the extent of violating Latin vocabulary and syntax![1] Tertullian in his many and varied works shows a good knowledge of both Old and New Testaments. Yet we can only speak of exegetical writings in any real sense with Hippolytus of Rome, in the early decades of the 3rd century, and it is symptomatic that he only expresses himself in Greek: proof of a training directed decisively towards Greek culture, whether in a Christian or pagan context.

Among the titles of his works engraved on the famous statue,[2] there are some of an exegetical nature, including the less than clear *Odes on all the Scriptures,* and a work on the Psalms. Under his name we have a fairly long text which includes an Introduction to the Psalter and the beginning of a commentary on Pss. 1 and 2.[3] The Introduction deals with the titles of the Psalms in a strongly allegorical manner: the 72 cantors are a symbol of the whole economy of mankind; the title, 'on the Heiress' refers to the Church; that 'on the eighth', to the day of judgment (pp. 169-171ff., Nautin). Still on the basis of titles, Hippolytus divides the Psalms among various authors (David, Asaph, the sons of Korah, etc.) and he explains the attribution of the entire Psalter to David, in terms of David's work of directing and organisation (p. 171). Both Ps. 1 and Ps. 2 are referred to Christ, the first to his birth and the second to his passion (p. 183).

In Western Christian literature after Hippolytus, by now entirely in Latin, interest in Scripture appears in different ways. Novatian in his *De Cibis Iudaicis* develops the traditional argument that the Jews were mistaken in understanding the Law literally rather than spiritually, and interprets some dietary regulations spiritually, as Ps.-Barnabas, had already done. Cyprian, in his *Testimonia ad Quirinum* has left us a large collection of *Testimonia* arranged by content according to their controversial, doctrinal and also (Bk. lll) disciplinary and moral ends. Some homilies of Ps.-Cyprian *De Centesima, De Montibus Sina et Sion*, develop scriptural themes in a moralistic and polemical context. But to encounter specifically exegetical works, we must move to the end of the 3rd and the beginning of the 4th century, with Victorinus of Pettau and Reticius of Autun.

Of the former, apart from the *Commentary on the Apocalypse* with which we shall deal shortly, we have a long fragment from the *De Fabrica Mundi*, in which the account of creation, taken in a literal sense, is ornamented with numerical symbolical references: the four elements of the world recall the four seasons of the year, the four Gospels, and the four rivers of paradise; the seventh day recalls the seventh millennium, in the millenarian sense (PL 5, 304, 309). All of this seems rather ingenuous and primitive to us especially if we consider that Victorinus was almost contemporary with Eusebius.

The *Commentary on the Song of Songs* by Reticius stands on much the same level. We know little about him other than Jerome's hostile judgment (*Ep.* 37). Among other things, he blames Reticius for not having consulted Origen's commentary on the Song of Songs. In effect, both Victorinus and Reticius present a cultural face of an Asiatic character (materialism, millenarianism, etc.) and do not seem to have been influenced in any appreciable way by Origen.

After these two pioneers, we have to move to the second half of the 4th century, to encounter true exegetical activity on a large scale. Perhaps it is not out of place to suppose that such prolonged lack of interest was if not caused, at least accentuated by, the very low opinion which many educated people had concerning the wretched Latin of translations of Scripture, and which they tried to offset by poetic paraphrases (Juvencus and others) which were more popular in the West than in the East. However, in the second half of the century, every obstacle seems to have been removed. Now under the auspices of Hilary and Marius Victorinus, and as a result of the notable cultural advancement which the Arian controversy forced on a sluggish West, exegesis gradually met with greater favour in the most diverse environments, until it became a fashionable cultural activity. As Jerome says: 'On the Scriptures, everyone quite indiscriminately undertakes some enterprise on his own account... the old gossip, the old fool, the wordy sophist, all of them take it up and tamper with it, teaching others before they learn themselves' (*Ep.* 53:7).

Obviously all this amateur nonsense has not come down to us, even if sometimes it was put into writing. The large amount of surviving literature, although displaying sometimes quite notably different standards among the various texts, is on the whole quite good. Obviously, the influence of Greek models was a determining factor, both for form and for content. Homilies (*tractatus, sermones*), on scriptural themes spread widely, sometimes preached as complete series in the style of Origen and Chrysostom (Ambrose, Augustine). But the systematic commentary also finds a niche of its own, at times achieving a remarkable length (Hilary, Ambrosiaster, Jerome, Augustine). Neither is the form of *Quaestiones* neglected, featuring passages of particular interest and gathered together in a more or less systematic series (Ambrosiaster, Jerome, Augustine).

With regard to exegetical method, Western authors with rare exceptions (Jerome) felt little need to deal with philological or historical questions which received so much attention in the East. When we turn to the manner of interpreting the biblical text, we notice a fairly widespread tendency towards allegorical interpretation, but a variety of attitudes and diverse reservations. Here the influence of Origen was decisive. Hilary, even before being exiled in Asia, had made a commentary on Matthew which was predominately allegorical but not specifically in the style of Origen; in the East, he came into contact with the works of this Alexandrian and was converted to both his spiritualism and his exegetical technique. His *Commentary on the Psalms* is merely a re-working of Origen's commentary which stays very close to the original. His *De Mysteriis* presents a series of traditional christological and ecclesial typologies (Adam and Eve, Abel, Joshua and Rahab), interpreted on the basis of the most typical Alexandrian criteria (symbolism of numbers, interpretation of Hebrew names, etc.). Ambrose also, who will sometimes let himself be inspired by Hippolytus (*De Patriarchis*), takes Origen as a primary source, alongside another Alexandrian, Philo. In fact, Ambrose, whose exegesis takes the form exclusively of preaching, has chiefly pastoral interests, and Alexandrian spiritual allegorism is for him congenial and easily developed along ascetic, moral and exhortatory lines. He has a particular interest in Old Testament episodes which are not usually studied, but which supply ample opportunities to condemn abuse of wealth and excessive attachment to it (*De Nabuthe, De Tobia*).

Apart from his numerous Old Testament commentaries, his *Expositio in Lucam* (which also makes room for literal interpretation) shows his preference for allegory. Ambrose normally distinguishes between the literal, moral and mystical (spiritual) senses, but like Origen, gives greatest importance to the last. In fact 'the mystical reading is the one which displays, in every part of Scripture, the totality of the action of a God who is pre-existent, within history and beyond history. This global vision was introduced by Christ with the categories of *spiritus* and "fulness", which point to the homogeneity of the Word of God as a whole and its concentration and summary in a typically Christian reading which reviews and completes all the previous levels' (Pizzolato).

The translations of Origen's homilies and commentaries by Jerome and Rufinus extended the influence of Alexandrian exegesis to areas where Greek was no longer known, with the result that Origen became very popular. The earliest commentaries of Jerome are little more than hasty paraphrases of Origen, and Rufinus, in his *De Benedictionibus Patriarcharum*, gives a perfect specimen of Origenistic interpretation: taking Gen. 49 systematically, first according to the literal sense, then the mystical (typological) sense and finally the moral (psychological) sense. However, the development of the Origenist controversy had the effect of tempering enthusiasm for the Alexandrian, even in the domain of exegesis. This then provided an opening for the requirements of a more 'modern' reading of Scripture, which we have seen already long established in various Eastern settings. Both Jerome and Augustine moderated their initial allegorising exploits considerably, but without ever reaching a purely literal reading of the sacred text.

Marius Victorinus had already begun an exegetical approach to the Pauline letters, which was strictly literal and would achieve great success, as we will see. But outside this specific area, the Antiochene style of exegesis had little impact in the West. Its most important advocate was Julian of Eclanum: his disdain for tradition, which at times inspired him to adopt revolutionary positions – as for example his exaltation of concupiscence in the controversy over the relation of grace and free will – suggested to him a form of reading Scripture which he felt to be quite modern, i.e. literal. Here he was decisively influenced by Theodore of Mopsuestia whom he also resembled in his doctrine of free will, and with whom he had taken refuge for a time during his wanderings in the East to escape the wrath of Augustine.[4] His surviving commentaries on Job and on three of the Minor Prophets (Hosea, Joel and Amos) are strictly literal. The second, in the tiny margin it allows to christological interpretation of the prophetic text follows strictly to the exegetical criteria of Theodore. In the Introduction to this Commentary Julian defines Origen's style of allegory as *lepida* ('charming') and charges Jerome with taking a half-way stance between literalism and allegorism in his commentary on the three prophets, with the result that he follows either Origen's allegory or the *fabulosae* traditions of the Jews, neglecting that which might usefully have appeared in the commentary (CCL 88, 116). The very few fragments still remaining from the *Commentary on the Song of Songs* certainly demonstrate an adherence to the traditional Christ/Church typology, but he also uses the 'erotic' element in the biblical text to set out his ideas on the positive evaluation of earthly love (CCL 88, 398ff.).

The Arians too carried on a notable exegetical activity between the end of the 4th century and the first decades of the 5th century, and their extant texts show the same oscillations between different styles of interpretation as seen in the catholic ones. The *Anonymus in Iob*, a commentary on Job, 1:1–3:19, while seeing Job as a *typos* of the suffering Christ, remains very sparing in the use of allegory and prefers the literal interpretation, with a certain interest in moral aspects. On the other hand, the vast commentary on Matthew, known as *Opus Imperfectum in Matthaeum*, favours the Alexandrian style of allegory to develop strongly existential themes, with the aim of encouraging the Arians to endure 'persecution' to which they are subjected by the now dominant catholics.

In this great flowering of Latin exegetical literature in the final decades of the 4th and first decades of the 5th century, there are many respectable figures beside the outstanding representatives: Gregory of Elvira, Zeno of Verona, Chromathius, and so on, the first two more interested in Old Testament themes, the third more attracted to Gospel topics (as far as our knowledge goes), but all three showing a tendency to connect both dispensations together, on the basis of an interpretation which is often allegorical for the New Testament and always for the Old Testament, sometimes with highly archaic touches in the typological treatment of people and events in the Old Testament.

Given the scope of this study, we can pass them over here, as we have partly done for writers of the first rank like Hilary and Ambrose, limiting a more detailed treatment to the few whose exegetical activity is particularly significant, either for its originality, or the more general impact of certain aspects of their exegesis.

2. *Marius Victorinus. Limited Knowledge of the Old Testament; Interest in Paul*

The famous grammarian Marius Victorinus, who converted to Christianity very late in life, wrote a commentary on certain letters of Paul after the year 360.[5] He had no Latin precedents to follow and he did not trouble to consult the Greek texts, such as those of Origen on the subject. His specifically Christian formation was indeed rather meagre. On becoming a Christian, Marius Victorinus brought to his new state in life the cultural baggage which he had acquired as a pagan, both philosophical and literary and he made this training the foundation of his Christian literary activity. In his commentaries on Paul, although the neo-platonic scholar appears from time to time, it is above all the grammarian who comes to the fore, the teacher accustomed to expounding Cicero and Virgil.

Each commentary is prefaced by a brief introduction, in which the author explains the motives which Paul had in writing that particular letter, and then gives a summary of it. There follows the systematic commentary, based on an attentive critical reading of the text, for which Victorinus, unusually among Western exegetes, uses more than one Latin edition and even occasionally refers to the Greek text. To make the total meaning of the texts in question easier to grasp, he gives a summary preview, which he then sharpens and deepens in the explanation details. Where the Pauline text gives an opportunity, Marius Victorinus does not evade doctrinal openings, but his own interest lies in the literal understanding of the text. Where Paul himself uses allegory, e.g. Gal. 4:22ff., the exegete explains the allegory briefly, but does not seize on it to allow the type of extensive development favoured by interpreters of an Alexandrian bent. This attitude is best seen, not as an allegiance to the anti-allegorical reaction which we have seen at work in various regions of the East in the 4th century, but rather as a transference by Marius Victorinus into the Christian domain of the interpretative criteria which he had for so long employed in his literal reading of the pagan classics.

It was just his great experience in this work and his habit of adhering strictly to the sense of the authors he explained, which permitted Marius Victorinus to grasp the development of Paul's thought in each individual letter, on the basis of the summary which prefaced it. Thus, the commentary on Galatians is set in the context of Paul's argument against Jewish legal observances with a tone that betrays an obvious anti-Jewish *animus*.

Still keeping close to the Pauline text, here and elsewhere our author insists strongly on the theme of justification by faith, seen as a gift of divine grace. The downgrading of good works (the recollection of which might deceive us about our non-existent merits) should be seen in the context of a Platonising interpretation of the Pauline opposition between faith and works as an opposition between intellectual, or contemplative, and practical activity. For Marius Victorinus, what is essential for salvation is a knowledge of the mystery which Paul mentions particularly in Ephesians. This mystery, which for Paul represents the salvific plan of God for the world through the redeeming work of Christ becomes, for Victorinus, immersed in the Arian controversy, the mystery of the generation of the Son by the Father and of the creation of the world through Christ (PL 8, 1265ff.).

Reading the commentaries of Marius Victorinus on Paul leads us to two further considerations of a more general nature. The first is suggested by his declaration that the Father of Christ *longe separatus est a deo Iudaeorum* (PL 8, 1247), a claim which smacks of Gnosticism and Manichaeism, and is unacceptable to any catholic. The fact is that Marius Victorinus' knowledge of the Old Testament was very, very limited. If we move back in time a little, the work of Lactantius would give rise to a fairly similar declaration. It would not be too risky a hypothesis to suggest that Lactantius' knowledge of the Old Testament was restricted to the passages contained in Cyprian's *Testimonia ad Quirinum*. These observations would seem to contrast with the interest in the Old Testament, so prevalent in comparison with the New Testament in various preachers of the 4th century: Gregory of Elvira, Zeno of Verona, Ambrose. The Manichaean controversy seems to have had little effect on this interest. And so we ask ourselves whether it might not be connected with our observation above, about the scant knowledge of the Old Testament even in people of some standing and might not demonstrate a need to compensate through preaching for ignorance which was sensed to be widespread among the faithful, and to which, among people with some education, the difficulties stemming from a literal reading of the Old Testament contributed.

The second consideration stems from the actual object of Marius Victorinus' exegetical interest: the letters of Paul. Indeed this commentary on Paul marks the beginning of a real flourishing of similar works, which in Rome, and in circles variously connected with Rome during the final decades of the 4th and the beginning of the 5th century, sees the commentary of Marius Victorinus joined by those of Ambrosiaster,[6] and Pelagius, the anonymous commentary contained in a Budapest codex,[7] the commentary of Jerome on certain Pauline letters, the loose translation by Rufinus of Origen's *Commentary on Romans* and the marked interest of Augustine for this same letter, even if this was never expressed in a systematic and complete commentary.[8] While the works by Rufinus and Jerome, closely dependent on Origen, are largely allegorising, the other three commentaries are of obviously literalist character. But apart from the differing hermeneutical criterion, all these works are connected by a common basic interest, and convergence of so many writings from the same time and place on Paul cannot be considered accidental. Among the various Pauline epistles, the greatest interest was concentrated on Romans, which demonstrates the doctrinal basis of such interest. It is an interest in the problem of justification and salvation: whether this results from the exercise of free human will, or whether it is from an external necessitating cause (*tyche*, fate, predestination, divine providence). The topic had been widely debated among Christians in the 2nd and 3rd centuries, in the Gnostic controversy, and in the period which concerns us here it had been revived, not only in the Manichaean dispute, but also through the spread of ascetic ideals, such as those of Pelagius, which, making total demands of the individual, needed a solid doctrinal basis. Such a base, no-one in Scripture could supply better than the Pauline letters. This, then, was the incentive for systematic study.

For our present purposes, the content of the interpretation is not important. It will be enough to observe that in those passages of Paul which concern problems of freedom and predestination, the interpretations reflect the differing points of view of the various authors, or in the specific case of Augustine, the diverse phases of his anguished change of mind: the same passages (e.g. Rom. 9:11ff.) which in the *Expositio 84 Propositiorum ex Epistola ad Romanos* (394) are interpreted in such a way as to safeguard the exercise of human free will (60, 62), a little later in the *De Diversis Quaestionibus ad Simplicianum* so as to emphasise the determining weight of God's grace and the inscrutability of his judgment (1, 2).

Sometimes doctrinal concern leads to an actual forcing of the reading: while Ambrosiaster interprets Rom. 9:16 ('So it depends not upon man's will or exertion, but upon God's mercy') so as to safeguard a margin of autonomy for the freedom of human action without forcing the text (CSEL 81, 318ff.), Pelagius, for the same reason, suggests reading the text as a question rather than a negative (PLS 1, 1153f.).

3. *Tyconius and the Interpretation of Revelation*

The first treatise on biblical hermeneutics which we have knowledge of in the West, the *Liber Regularum*, was written by the African Tyconius, a Donatist active between 370 and 390 who found himself embroiled in controversy not only with the catholic party, but also with the Donatists themselves. The book makes no claim to be a general treatise, as was Origen's treatment in *De Princ.* IV 1-3, and as Augustine's *De Doctrina Christiana* soon would be. Here, the intention was rather to offer the key to clarify the *recessus* which keep hidden the treasures of the truth (PL 18, 15). All seven rules (which almost always presuppose allegorical interpretation), are extremely acute[9] and they all deserve to be set out, however briefly.

The first, *de domino et corpore eius*, explains that when Scripture refers to Christ, it does not distinguish between him and his body, i.e. the Church, but moves indiscriminately from one to the other. The stone cut from the mountain which annihilates the kingdoms of the world (Dan. 2:34) is a figure of Christ, but when it becomes a mountain, which fills the whole earth, it specifically prefigures the Church.

The second rule, *de domini corpore bipartito*, explains that Scripture refers to the Church as to a body formed of two parts, one of good people, the other of wicked: thus in the Song of

Songs 1:4; the bride says 'I am black, but lovely,' and Paul speaks of *inimici* and *dilecti* together (Rom. 11:28).

The third rule, *de promissis et lege*, explains the apparent contradiction of passages in Romans and Galatians where the Law of Moses is sometimes presented positively and sometimes negatively, by appealing to the progress between the new and old dispensation, i.e. from the Law to faith, and recalls the educational function of the Law (Gal. 3:24).[10]

The fourth rule, *de genere et specie*, explains mainly on the basis of prophetic texts, that Scripture sometimes passes from species to genus, i.e. from the part to the whole and vice-versa. The various towns and peoples named in the Old Testament are figures of the Church, sometimes of the entire Church (= the whole) sometimes only of the good part or the bad part (= the part).

The fifth rule, *de temporibus*, uses synecdoche (the part for the whole and vice-versa) to propose a solution of certain apparent contradictions in chronological calculations in Scripture, e.g. the contradiction between Gen. 15:13 (the Jewish people will be oppressed in Egypt for 400 years) and Ex. 12:40 (the Jewish people will dwell in Egypt for 430 years), contradictions which result from the fact that the people were not oppressed for every single year of their stay in Egypt.

The sixth rule, *de recapitulatione*, explains that Scripture sometimes locates in one significant moment a concept which has a much wider time reference: the eschatological warnings of Matt. 24:15-18 and Lk. 17:30ff. are not only valid for the actual moment of the second coming of Christ, but should be observed at all times.

The last rule, *de diabolo et corpore eius*, corresponds to the first: when Scripture refers to the devil, it includes equally his body, i.e. those who belong to him. For example, when Isaiah speaks of Lucifer's fall from heaven (14:12ff.) the mention of all the kings and all the nations should be referred to the body of the devil.

Even before writing this work, Tyconius had written a commentary on Revelation, which marked a turning point in Western interpretation of this difficult text. Earlier, we touched on the fact that the Millenarians based their convictions on a literal interpretation of chapters 20 and 21 of Revelation, and that in controversy with them Origen had given an entirely spiritual interpretation to these chapters. In the dispute with Nepos, Dionysius, without explicitly invalidating the authority of the Revelation,[11] underlined the difficulty of interpreting it. As a consequence of this controversy, and of the predominance of Alexandrian culture over that of Asia, the Book of Revelation was largely neglected in the East.

In the West, Millenarianism took longer to die, and it is to one such millenarian, Victorinus of Pettau, whose *De Fabrica Mundi* we have already mentioned, that we owe the first known commentary on Revelation. It is a rather short work which does not explain every single verse and explains what it does succinctly. The markedly symbolical nature of the biblical text encourages the development of allegorical interpretation, quite apart from the allegory of the text itself. While Victorinus respects the intentions of the author when he sees the Church in the 'woman' of chap. 12, and the Roman Empire in the beast in chap. 13 (PLS 1, 149,155), he oversteps the symbolism of the text when he interprets the lightning, voices thunder of Rev. 4:5; as divine preaching, the coming of the Lord, and the writings of the New Testament, and when he sees the Holy Spirit represented in the eagle of Rev. 8:13 (126, 140). But despite this allegorising tendency, he gives a strictly literal interpretation of the resurrection of the righteous, the thousand year reign and the new Jerusalem of Rev. 20:21 (164ff.). Precisely for this reason, towards the end of the 4th century with Millenarianism declining now also in the West, Jerome, who had great respect and admiration for his literary fellow countryman, decided to revise his commentary with the main intention of amending any Millenarian references: in this revision, the millennial reign is neither millennial or earthly, and the new Jerusalem becomes the company of all the saints (PLS 1, 166, 168).

Between Victorinus and Jerome, comes the *Commentary on the Apocalypse* by Tyconius.[12] This interpretation, decidedly allegorical and spiritualising, has the chief aim of illustrating the relationship between Christ and the Church.[13] The latter, in keeping with the Tyconius' basic line of thought[14] is seen in the most varied figures: the angels of Rev. 2:19; 8:2, 6; 10:10; 11:18; the new Jerusalem of 3:12; the altar of 8:3; the elders of 9:7; the lamps of 11:4; the woman clothed with the sun of 12:1 (Christ is the sun, the apostles, the crown of twelve stars; heretics, the moon under the woman's feet (PLS 1, 649)). But Tyconius' major innovation was to broaden the eschatological dimension of the Johannine text, extending it to signify not only the last times but the whole period of the Church's life. In this perspective, any Millenarian implication vanished, and the anti-Roman *animus* of the biblical text took on a notably different complexion.[15]

Tyconius' interpretation affected all later Western exegesis of Revelation decisively. Jerome took inspiration from it in his revision of Victorinus' work; Augustine also kept it before him, even if he never wrote a commentary on this text. The African Primasius of Hadrumetum, who wrote in the middle of the 6th century, claims in the preface to his wide-ranging *Commentary on the Apocalypse*, to have been inspired by both Augustine and the Donatist Tyconius whose commentary he has purged of anti-catholic touches, convinced that, for the good of the Church, one should look not at personalities but rather at the quality of what they write. His basic structure is that of Tyconius, but compared to his source, the final though obvious references to the Roman Empire are eliminated: the beast of chap. 13 indicates Rome, yes, but this is taken as a symbol of all earthly powers, in the same way that the seven churches named at the beginning of the work symbolise the entire Church, this last feature certainly deriving from Tyconius. The woman who is seated on the beast becomes a symbol of all sinners. The first resurrection of the righteous is that *per fidem* and the millennial reign is the entire life-span of the Church (PL 68, 797, 899f., 914, 917).

The Spanish writer Apringius of Beja, almost contemporary with Primasius, betraying in his commentary on Revelation more or less the same influences, shows himself to be the author of a commentary which has erroneously come down to us under the name of Augustine, but which might be taken as the work of Caesarius of Arles. And even in the 8th century the influence of Tyconius can be detected in the Anglo-Saxon

Bede, in the Italianised Frank Ambrose Autpert, and in the Spanish Beatus of Liebana, our main source for the reconstruction of the major, lost, proportion of Tyconius' work.

4. *Jerome*

Jerome's first serious contact with Scripture was through the works of Origen, and his earliest commentaries (around 386) mainly devoted to Paul,[16] are little more than paraphrases of Origen, combined with touches from Didymus and Apollinaris. Jerome re-echoes even the more contested doctrines of Origen, the pre-existence of souls, and final apocatastasis (PL 26, 485f.). When he was accused of relying too heavily on Origen, he defended himself both by referring back to famous Latin literary figures who had drawn upon Greek models, Ennius, Plautus, Terence, Cicero and even Hilary (PL 25, 1189f.) and by claiming that commentaries only intended to present different interpretations of Scripture passages which were difficult to interpret, so that the reader could judge which is more true, and like a good money-changer reject false coin (PL 23, 428). In effect his initial preoccupation at this early stage of his exegetical activity was to put the Latin reader in contact with the treasures of Eastern exegesis, to put Origen into Latin and make him available for Roman ears (PG 13, 655). Jerome sets about this task either by direct translation, or transposing into Latin, in his own name, Origen and other Greek commentators, availing himself of the traditional indulgence which the Latins had always accorded to their writers for their flamboyant renditions from Greek.[17]

But his contact with Origen had the result, above all, of refining Jerome's critical faculties, which we must suppose had already been trained in the Roman school of the grammarian Donatus, and of familiarising him with the philological and archaeological aspects of Origen's exegesis. The fruits of this first philological and archaeological approach to the scriptural text are found in his reworking of lists of geographical and personal names in Scripture, which Eusebius and others had translated into Greek and edited together with essential information (*Liber locorum, Liber nominum*), and in his collection of *Quaestiones* on Genesis which scoured Origen's *Hexapla* to explain certain expressions in the sacred text. But by far the most important outcome of this philological activity was the production of the Latin translation of the Old Testament, made directly from the Hebrew (c. 398-405). The decision to undertake this demanding task was of great importance, because the Greek Septuagint was not only the official text of the Old Testament for the Eastern Church, but even considered to have been divinely inspired itself, and the translations in use in the West adhered very closely to it. Jerome's decision was encouraged by contact with Origen's Hexapla, which, setting the Septuagint side by side with other translations, showed up its limitations and defects. For a Greek reader the Hexapla, or more simply the Tetrapla, or the text of the Septuagint accompanied by marginal notations of variants from other translations were enough for a critical reading of the Old Testament text, but it was quite impossible to transfer Origen's complex instrument straightforwardly into Latin. So anyone who wished to supply the Latin reader with a reliable text of the Old Testament would have to break away from the Septuagint and have direct recourse to the original texts. Jerome's great merit was to have understood and satisfied this need, even though his restricted knowledge of Hebrew obliged him to rely heavily on Aquila and Symmachus as well.

The undertaking of this translation coincided more or less with the outbreak of the controversy over Origen, which saw Jerome sensationally abandon the master whom till then he had idolised. The position in which he now found himself as a result of this about-turn was particularly difficult. To those who reproached him for his past Origenist sins, Jerome defended himself as best could by distinguishing the *dogmatistes* in Origen from the *interpres*, i.e. the exegete and claiming that he had followed only the latter. In fact, during the controversy, he began to disassociate himself even from the hermeneutical criteria of Origen, and to listen to the new criteria which the Antiochenes were proposing and especially making fuller use of the philological and linguistic component of interpretation.

But it was never his intention to adhere totally to Antiochene criteria, and his detachment from Origen was really only partial, taking him to a middle position which, given too the haste with which he usually worked, easily lost coherence. On the one hand, he reiterates the typically Antiochene criticism of the arbitrariness of allegorical interpretation, by which exegetes, without considering what the prophets and apostles really say, adjust disagreeable texts to suit their own view (*Ep.* 53:7); but on the other hand, he often reaffirms the validity of Origen's threefold division of scriptural meanings, historical, moral and spiritual, referring to Prov. 22:20, which we have already seen Origen use to this end (PL 25, 147, 1027),[18] because the literal historical meaning of the prophetic texts[19] is not simple but full of enigmas since one thing speaks in the words, another is contained in the sentences (PL 24, 629).

We can illustrate this method of interpretation in Jerome from the *Commentary on Jonah*. Shortly after the beginning, he objects to the claim that the historical sense and the spiritual sense (*tropology*) always run together in Scripture: Paul gave an allegorical interpretation to Sarah and Hagar, but not every detail of that story can be taken allegorically. In the same way not everything in the biblical account of the creation of man can be interpreted in terms of the Pauline typology (Eph. 5:31f.) Adam/Eve – Christ/Church. Thus also not everything in the Jonah story can be applied to Christ on the basis of the Christ/Jonah relationship established in Matt. 12:39f. (PL 25, 1123f.). It is precisely the same principle which, a few years later, Cyril was to formulate in relation to the same Old Testament book. But while we have seen that Cyril applies the principle coherently, the same cannot be said of Jerome. He does indeed reject the allegorical interpretation of certain details in the text, but this type of interpretation according to the rules of Alexandrian hermeneutics is by far his preferred approach: note at the very beginning, the allegory based on the etymology of the name Jonah (1120f.). Jerome's adherence to Origen's model is so close that he actually develops downright reckless interpretations of the kind which Antiochenes attacked most fiercely: Jonah fleeing from the presence of God and going to Tarshish (Jon. 1:3), on the basis of the etymology of Tarshish (= sea), is taken to be a *typos* of Christ who through his incarnation abandoned his heavenly homeland and, as it were, fled from the heavenly realms to go to Tarshish, i.e. the sea of this world; the embarkation at Joppa, a city of Judah symbolises the fact that Christ came in the first instance to save the Jews, voyaging through storms at sea, i.e. through his passion and death (PL 25, 1122f.). In this commentary, written at the height of the Origenist controversy (396), the atmosphere is one hundred per cent Origenist.

The last commentaries on the Minor Prophets (Zechariah, Malachi, Hosea, Joel, Amos) and those on Isaiah, Jeremiah, Ezekiel and Daniel, which occupied Jerome from 405 till his death (419) are the fully mature fruit of an exegetical method which makes ample use of earlier authors, and without being excessively slow, examines the text of the prophets from philological-linguistic, historical and spiritual points of view. The fact that he had concentrated his own interests exclusively on the prophets allowed Jerome – as we saw earlier in Eusebius – to give a christological interpretation of the sacred text without having recourse to the forced excesses which the Antiochenes criticised in the Alexandrians. However, this determination to maintain a middle position between the literalist excesses of Diodorus and the excessive allegorism of Origen[20] gives Jerome's exegesis, like that of Cyril, a touch of something desultory. By this is meant that too often allegory appears unexpectedly and without any cogent reason; it is merely the result of a passing suggestion in a particular source, usually Origen or Didymus. For example, in the interpretation of Is. 7:3-4, Jerome gives the etymological meaning of Shear-Jashub (remnant and returning) and uses this to make him a *typos* of the people of Judah (PL 24, 103); in his commentary on Ezek. 4:16-17, the want of bread in Jerusalem becomes a symbol of the want of spiritual bread and water in the Church (PL 25, 50). This method of drawing freely on diverse sources (PL 25, 820) and intertwining a Christian spiritual interpretation (*tropologian nostrorum*: PL 25, 1418) with the history of the Jews does not help to add to the general coherence of Jerome's commentaries.

Neither does Jerome's only gospel commentary on Matthew escape this charge. Indeed, in an interpretation which purports to be deliberately literalist, despite its brevity there is no lack of allegorical readings, obviously inherited from Origen. A comparison of the two miracles of feeding (Matt. 14:13ff.; 15:29ff.), entirely constructed on numerical considerations (in the one 5 and 12, and in the other, 7 and 4) emphasises the superiority of the second feeding over the first (PL 26, 116). In the account of Jesus' entry into Jerusalem (Matt. 21:1ff.) we note the etymology of the name, Bethphage (= House of Jews) but above all the observation that Jesus could not have sat simultaneously on an ass and a foal; the impossibility of the literal sense leads to the allegory: ass = Jews; foal = pagans (PL 26, 152ff.). On the whole, Jerome's exegetical work is more impressive for its philological rigour and the abundance of materials used than for coherence of method or originality of interpretation.

5. *Augustine*

Both in his theory and practice, Augustine's exegesis shows traces of his own unfortunate introduction to Scripture and of the episodes that followed: his initial distaste as a young student for the rough and ready quality of the Latin translations of the Bible; his joining the Manichees, whose aversion to the Old Testament explained certain anthropomorphisms of Genesis and Exodus; his return to the catholic understanding of Scripture, thanks to hearing Ambrose's allegorical exegesis of the Old Testament, and to his embracing Platonism, which found theoretical backing in this kind of exegesis. After his conversion, as Augustine became ever more involved in the life of the Church, he devoted himself with greater application to the study of Scripture, finally making it both the basis and the content of authentic Christian culture. His numerous scriptural works, whether in the form of commentary, homily, or *quaestio*, show this progressive deepening also in the area of exegetical method.

Immediately after his conversion, either through the example of Ambrose, or as a result of the Manichean controversy, Augustine was strongly allegorist. As he gradually became aware of what seemed to many the arbitrary exaggerations of this exegesis he withdrew to more moderate positions which coincided by and large – and so far as they are specifically

104 *Biblical Interpretation in the Early Church*

concerned with the rationale of interpretation – with the positions of Jerome.[21] The most obvious difference between the two was that Augustine had a strong rhetorical sensitivity, and developed his exegesis principally in the service of his pastoral activity: this explains his scant interest in the fundamental critical and philological component of Jerome's exegesis. Augustine was very cold towards Jerome's translation of the Old Testament directly from the Hebrew and his exaltation of *hebraica veritas*; his own preaching systematically sought out pastoral opportunities so that the interpretation of the sacred text might provide spiritual nourishment for all, especially for the less well educated, who could only approach Scripture fruitfully by this means.

The evolution of Augustine's style of interpretation can be perfectly grasped from the different forms of exegesis which he gave to the first three chapters of the Book of Genesis. We have already pointed out the fundamental importance of this text for anthropology, and hence also for Christian soteriology. For this reason, Augustine returned to the interpretation of it on several occasions, from the *De Genesi adversus Manichaeos*, shortly after his conversion (389), to *De Genesi ad Litteram*, completed only around 415.[22] In the first work, he strives to overcome Manichaean objections relating to the anthropomorphisms of Scripture and to other disconcerting aspects of the text of Genesis, making vigorous use of allegory which is theoretically justified by the traditional observation that certain details of the text are not explicable at the literal level (II 2:3). In truth, Augustine claims himself disposed to admire the person who can explain a text in the literal manner alone; but he continues that where no conclusion is given, in order to understand the text in a manner worthy of God, one needs to consider figuratively and in riddles.

The Augustine of this work often reminds us of the passage in which Eusebius of Emesa accuses allegorists of resorting to this style of exegesis purely because of their inability to interpret the text adequately in a literal manner. With the passage of time, and with the refinement of his scriptural sensitivity, Augustine convinces himself of this very idea, and in his *De Genesi ad Litteram*, he explicitly retracts his earlier declaration, claiming that he had been unable to meet the Manichaean objections in any other way, whereas now he continues – I think I can explain the texts in question according to the proper, not the allegorical exposition (VII 2:5). One should not think, however, even if the title suggests it, that this is a purely literal interpretation: Augustine makes it clear that the biblical account of creation and of sin is not figurative like the Song of Songs, but it is history; *sui generis,* so as to require allegorical interpretation (VII 1:2). The interpretation of the two trees in paradise, about which he makes the following observations, shows his new way of interpreting the biblical text.

In *De Genesi adversus Manichaeos,* he had interpreted the tree of life as an allegory of wisdom and the tree of knowledge as an allegory of the moderation and integrity of the soul (II 9:12). Now he interprets the two trees as two real trees; the first is a symbol of Christ, while the second is significant not for the fruit that it bears, but for the consequence of transgressing the prohibition to eat it (VIII 4:8). Basically the Augustine of *De Genesi ad Litteram,* is not *a priori* anti-allegorist; in fact his commentary gives ample space to allegorical interpretation as, for example, the lengthy passage on the symbolism of the days of creation amply illustrates (IV 1ff.). He does, however, shrink from those excesses which, in the name of allegory, sometimes deny the literal meaning of the text.

Among his lesser non-homiletic works intended to illustrate the Old Testament, we should recall particularly the *In Heptateuchum Locutiones,* which recall much later the preoccupation of the young Augustine with linguistic purity. In this he explains countless expressions in the early Latin translations which sounded harsh to educated readers, as a result of remaining too close to the Greek or Hebrew mode of expression and turns them into better Latin, or at least clarifies their meaning.

It has already been stated that much of Augustine's exegetical activity was pastorally orientated in the form of sermons; given that he concerned himself, like no-one else in his time, with how best to communicate with listeners of minimal learning, his exegesis too displays this same primary concern.

Amd so in his *sermones*, we encounter the most elementary hermeneutical observations. The Old Testament is the figurative promise, while the New Testament is the promise understood in the spiritual sense (*Serm.* 4:7). The same entities do not always have the same allegorical meaning (for example, the mountain does not always signify the Lord etc.: *Serm.* 31:6), and one single entity can be signified in different ways (the lion is different from the lamb, but Our Lord can be represented by the one or the other: *Serm.* 4:25). We are in the ambit of the traditional typological and more generally allegorical reading of the Old Testament, the one best able to develop the text read in Church in such a way as to instruct the faithful and encourage them in Christian commitment. It is precisely this aim which structures the exegesis proper, in a procedure which often recalls the first of Tyconius' rules, in that Augustine moves easily from speaking of Christ to speaking of his body, the Church.

We cannot enter into these didactic and exhortatory aspects of Augustine's preaching here. It will be enough to remember that Augustine did not limit his preaching to texts chosen at random or determined by a particular liturgy, but also preached complete or very extensive sets of sermons. The *Enarrationes in Psalmos* and the *Tractatus in Iohannem*[23] are outstanding examples of this type of preaching, in which Augustine not only gives himself unstintingly to his pastoral ministry, but also shows his by now quite refined exegetical sensitivity. In the light of what we have said about Augustine's Old Testament exegesis in general, it will be obvious that he should have continued to interpret the Psalms in a broadly christological manner, exploiting the various devices which we noted earlier in Eusebius. Like Eusebius, Augustine also takes Pss. 44, 59, 68 and 79 to be christological on the strength of the *inscriptio* 'for those who will be changed'. But just this comparison with Eusebius on, for example, Ps. 69 brings out the particular qualities of Augustine's interpretation. In the sense indicated above, he refers the psalm to Christ not only as head but also as the body, i.e. the Church, while Eusebius' interpretation is narrowly christological. The frequent reference to the etymology of Hebrew names as a basis for allegorical interpretation is an eloquent demonstration of Augustine's adherence to the traditional structures of Alexandrian hermeneutics, see for example, at the beginning of Ps. 51, the attention given to the names Saul = request, desire; Doeg = movement; Edomite = terrain.

If, as we have already seen in the explanation of some points in Romans (cf. p. 95), Augustine can adhere to the literal interpretation for doctrinal reasons, the *Tractatus in Iohannem* shows how willingly he turns to allegorical interpretation where his purpose is less technical than elsewhere, and attempts to give his listeners a lesson in total Christianity. To this extent allegory could serve to introduce exhoratory considerations: the dealers in the Temple are a figure of those in the Church who seek their own interests rather than Christ, while the Christian ought not to be attached to earthly things (*Tract. in Jo.* 10:6); *pisticus* (= authentic), used of the ointment at Bethany (Jn. 12:3), is connected with *pistis* (= faith) to indicate that we should anoint the feet of Jesus by the way we live the faith (*Tract. in Jo.* 50:6).

The *De Doctrina Christiana,* devoted as it is to presenting Scripture as the foundation of Christian learning, is to a large extent a treatise on biblical hermeneutics, in which Augustine draws not only on his now mature exegetical experience, but also on his awareness of his limitations; as, for example, when he insists on the value to the exegete of knowing not only Greek (of which he himself knew little), but even Hebrew (II 11). The basic theme which underlies the whole work is the difficulty inherent in the interpretation of Scripture for which he gives the traditional reason 'to wear out pride with hard work and to keep intelligence from boredom' (II 6:7). From this is derived advice about the complex, initial training necessary for the exegete and also the assertion in the light of the principle that the fulness and also the end of Scripture is love, that any interpretation of Scripture which promotes love is acceptable, even if it was not in the intention of the sacred writer, while an interpretation which does not achieve this goal is mistaken (I 35-36). It follows that there is no danger in giving two or more interpretations of a difficult passage, provided that they find some backing elsewhere in Scripture (III 27:38), so that a clear passage helps to elucidate an obscure one (III 26:37). The concluding observation, that multiplicity of meanings for a single passage is intended by divine providence to increase the richness of the sacred text (III 27:38), seems to rehabilitate what we have seen to be the fundamental intuition of Origen's exegesis.

NOTES

[1] We can connect with the diffusion of Latin translations of Scripture the so-called Muratorian Fragment, a list of New Testament writings considered to be inspired, written in Rome towards the end of the 2nd century, and some anti-Marcionite prologues to the Gospels.

[2] We take this writer to be different from the author of *The Commentary on Daniel* and other related works, whom we have already discussed in chap. I, pp. 27-30; cf. note 22 to chap. I.

[3] Many exegetical fragments which have come to us under the name of Hippolytus are of doubtful authorship, given the uncertainty over the exact historical and literary identity of this person.

[4] Julian has also given us the Latin translation of Theodore's commentary on many Psalms.

[5] We have the commentaries on Ephesians, Galatians and Philippians but allusions imply that Victorinus also commented on Romans and on I and II Corinthians.

[6] To this enigmatic individual we also owe *Questiones Veteris et Novi Testamenti*, a treatise which reveals various interests doctrinal and disciplinary as well as strictly exegetical, worked out in a mostly, though not exclusively literalist manner.

[7] Cf. H. J. Frede, *Ein neuer Paulustext und Kommentar*, I-II, Freiburg 1973-74. Apart from Rome, the work could have been written at Aquileia, an environment closely connected with Rome through Jerome and Rufinus. The book also offers a brief commentary on the Letter to the Hebrews, the first in Latin, as far as we know, because it rarely appeared in any Western canon. In the East, on the other hand, Origen had already written a major commentary on it, now lost.

[8] Cf. the two works mentioned below. The second, replying to questions put by Simplicianus, Ambrose's successor in Milan, shows his own interest in problems of justification and free will.

[9] Augustine esteemed these so highly that he summarised them all at length in *De Doctrina Christiana* III 30-37.

[10] The second rule disputes the Donatist position that only good people make up the Church, and not sinners. The third rule also has anti-Donatist overtones, as well as anti-Manichean and anti-Gnostic.

[11] Such authority was challenged on different occasions in the first half of the 3rd century, following the anti-Montanist and anti-Millenarian reaction.

[12] The work as a whole has been lost. One manuscript from Turin has preserved certain excerpts relating to Revelation chapters 2, 3, 7, 8, 9, 10, 11, 12. The work can, however, be reconstructed from later commentaries deriving from it, particularly that of Beatus of Liebana.

[13.]Tyconius put his rules into practice: for the alternation genus/species, cf. 2:21-23; 12:1.

[14.]Here too Tyconius attacks the particularism of the Donatists who strive to make narrow the Church of God, which in fact has spread through the whole world and in which the good and the bad are mixed (3:9, 10, 12; 8:12).

[15.]We lack direct evidence of Tyconius' commentary on the most openly anti-Roman references of Revelation; to reconstruct it, we need to go to later commentaries, with the uncertainties that this involves.

[16.]Jerome wrote commentaries on Galatians, Ephesians, Titus and Philemon.

[17.]V. Peri (*Omilie origeniane sui Salmi*, Vatican City 1980) has recently shown that a series of homilies by Jerome on the Psalms is no more than an adaptation of Origen's homilies.

[18.]On this point, cf. also *Ep.* 120:12.

[19.]It should be remembered that from 393 onwards Jerome devoted his exegetical labours almost exclusively to commentaries firstly on the minor, then on the major prophets.

[20.]Jerome, recalling his sources in the introduction to individual commentaries, frequently points out that Origen and Didymus had given little attention to the literal interpretation of texts (PL. 25, 1418, 1543).

[21.]But Augustine was always much more inclined than Jerome to use hermeneutical procedures of the Alexandrian style, especially the symbolism of numbers.

[22.]Between these two works may be placed the *De Genesi Imperfectus Liber* and Books XI-XIII of the *Confessions*, which also feature the interpretation of Gen. 1-3.

[23.]In both collections some addresses were not actually preached before a congregation, but dictated to complete the commentary.

Chapter 5

Exegetical Literature from the 5th to the 6th Century

1. *The East*

In Alexandria, exegesis, like all other forms of cultural activity at any serious level, was heavily dependent on the vitality of the School and substantially on the vitality of the tradition handed down from Origen. This tradition certainly had its ups and downs, but it was preserved reasonably intact until the time of Didymus; but between the end of the 4th and the start of the 5th century it suffered both from the effects of the Origenist controversy and from the assault of Antiochene Literalism. Effectively, after Didymus, the School really lost all its importance in Alexandria and in Cyril, who does not seem to have had much connection with the School, Alexandrian exegesis followed a new path, sacrificing much of its traditional character. The progressive emergence of the autochthonous (Coptic) element following the Monophysite controversy was the decisive blow to this local Christian cultural tradition, which had drawn its most distinctive significance from a creative alliance with Greek culture.[1] The beginning of the crisis for the Alexandrian School coincided with the full blossoming of the Antiochene School, but this also suffered very severe side-effects from the christological controversy. It first saw accusations levelled against its leading exponents, living (Theodoret) or dead (Diodorus, Theodore) and immediately afterwards witnessed the appearance in Syria itself of one of the epicentres of Monophysitism, here too nourished by the local reaction against Hellenism. Thus, albeit for very different reasons, in the middle of the 5th century Christian learning was seriously in decline both in Alexandria and at Antioch; and the appearance of lesser centres of learning (Edessa, Nisibis and Gaza) could not recover much of this heritage.

Exegetical activity, especially understood as systematic, critical study of Scripture in the manner of Origen, Didymus, Diodorus or Theodore, was the first to feel the decline and the climate of intolerance and insecurity brought about by the christological controversy. Even if there was no lack of important figures or significant undertakings, the prevailing tendency was to refer back to the great exegetes of the past, rather than to try new ways, and a progressive sterility followed.

Among the leading figures, we might recall Gregory of Agrigentum (second half of the 6th century) who wrote an extensive commentary on Ecclesiastes. Setting out his method at the beginning of his text, he compares the superficial approach to Scripture to milk, while the greater consistency of butter represents the more penetrating and exacting approach (PG 98, 741). This is a typical opening which normally introduces allegorical interpretation and this impression is reinforced by the typology which follows, that of Solomon/Christ based on the etymology Solomon = 'peaceful' (745). But then the commentary becomes predominately literal, based on the obvious opposition between the transitoriness of worldly goods, highlighted by the author and the permanence of heavenly goods, an opposition which suits the moralising and exhortatory tone of the work. Not infrequently, however, there is a second level of meaning which is more specifically christological: 'The wise man's eyes are in his head' (Eccl. 2:14), recalls Christ, the head of his body, the Church; while the dead flies of Eccl. 10:1 anagogically signify the demons which settle in the rotten areas of the human soul (817,1089); often, a mention of bread is connected with the bread of the Eucharist (836,1072).

It is symptomatic that only in this late stage, a period of obvious weariness, do the first Greek commentaries on Revelation appear. We have already mentioned the vicissitudes of this book in the wake of the anti-Montanist and anti-Millenarian controversies. Even when Millenarianism was no more than a quaint memory, the book continued to be viewed with suspicion: quotations from it are few and far between, with the exception of perhaps Gregory of Nazianzus, and even its canonicity was hotly debated.[2] The two authors to whom we now turn, Oecumenius and Andrew of Caesarea (in Cappadocia), who followed one another at an uncertain date in the 6th or 7th century, still had to defend its canonicity against critics. Both of their commentaries, given the particular nature of the text which they were examining, were heavily allegorical; however, they display characteristics which distinguish them clearly from each other. Oecumenius, who is strongly influenced by Origen, interprets Revelation in a more broadly ecclesial rather than a narrowly eschatological sense, including present, past, and future, so that the text can be read on two levels: one referring to the incarnation of Christ, the other to the end of the world. The interpretation has traces of earlier works, but is developed in a personal manner quite free from any conditioning. Andrew's chief concern, on the other hand, is to strengthen the authority of Revelation with the testimony of authors of the golden age of the Church's history, and, without noticing his inconsistency, he quotes representatives of the Asiatic, millenarian tradition: Irenaeus, Hippolytus, Methodius, quite apart from Gregory of Nazianzus, Epiphanius and some others. He argues about the nature of the work with Oecumenius, without actually naming him, and opposes his more generous chronological reference with his own more rigid version which refers the text to the last times which, for him, are very near.

The interpretation of various details reflects this fundamental difference of approach. A few examples are enough to make the point. For Oecumenius, the woman pursued by the dragon in Rev. 12, is Mary who gives birth to Jesus (pp. 135ff., Hoskier) and this is the earliest Marian interpretation I have found for this particular passage;[3] on the other hand, while he notes this interpretation, Andrew immediately sets against it the more traditional view of the woman as the Church, appealing to a quotation from Methodius (PG 106, 319f.). For Oecumenius, the harlot who sits upon the beast is Rome, the great persecutor who drinks the blood of the martyrs (p. 184, Hoskier): the comparison between Rome and Constantinople, the New

Rome, becomes for him a comparison between pagan and Christian Rome. Andrew, on the other hand, challenges this interpretation and sees the woman as a symbol of earthly rule in general (PG 106, 373f.). Obviously neither of the two authors gives a literal interpretation of the thousand years of Rev. 20:2; Oecumenius gives the number 1000 a specific symbolic value and refers the 1000 years to the moment of Christ's incarnation (p. 215, Hoskier). Andrew rejects both the literal, millenarian interpretation and that of Oecumenius, and reads the 1000 years more generally: they refer to the period from the incarnation to the end of the world (PG 106, 409).

But the work which achieved greatest success in its day and signalled a turning point in exegetical activity in the East was the *Commentary on the Octateuch* by Procopius of Gaza (who wrote between the end of the 5th and the first decades of the 6th century). Procopius, in keeping with the tendencies of a time when doctrinal anthologies were becoming ever more popular, gave up at the outset any claim to originality, and in his extensive commentary, for each verse, gave verbatim extracts from many widely different earlier interpretations so that the reader had to hand a synthetic overview of patristic interpretation of the first books of the Old Testament. The size of the book, which must have made it difficult to handle, induced him to write an abridgement in which the various interpretations of individual texts from the several Books are summarised and grouped together according to their nature without any reference to names of authors. Only this second edition has come down to us,[4] but the first showed the way and first marked the flowering of similar works, known as *Catenae*.

Normally, a Catena was made by transcribing in the centre of the page the biblical text, and in all the margins one or more interpretations for each verse, preceded by the author's name in the genitive case: the extract may quote verbatim a significant passage from its source, or it may merely summarise it. This type of compilation soon became popular and decisively shaped exegesis for some time to come. Hence we have many anthologies of this kind often relating to the same biblical texts, but made by selecting material differing at least in part, from one collection to another. The material is still to some extent unedited. It is not always simple or reliable to use it, because sometimes the relationship of one catena to another is not too clear, and especially because attributions are often erroneous as a result of mistakes made in transcribing material from one copy to another. The material is, however, of great importance to the modern scholar, because only from tthis source can we know a little and sometimes more than a little about important exegetical works which have not come down to us directly and in their entirety. Just to give an example, almost all our knowledge on someone as important as Diodorus is solely from Catenae. It is beyond doubt, however, that the popularity of this kind of compilation contributed not a little to the decline in the use of complete commentaries of many authors and so to their disappearance.

In a period of decline, and hence of small intellectual commitment, manuals as well as anthologies are in demand; and we will complete this brief survey of Eastern exegesis in the 5th and 6th centuries by touching on the *Introduction to the Sacred Scriptures* by the little known Hadrianus, who may be placed more or less in the first half of the 6th century.[5] This short manual seeks to clarify certain important characteristics of the way things are expressed in the sacred books. The author explains with plentiful examples that the sacred writers often refer expressions to God which come from forms of speech determined by various aspects of the human condition: senses, limbs, passions and so on: so God is given a voice, a mouth; he is made to repent, to become angry and so on (PG 98, 1273ff.). Other peculiarities of the language used in Scripture can be explained as stylistic devices: washing one's hands means having nothing to do with a certain business; the number seven signifies abundance and perfection (1288, 1292). Still other peculiarities are explained on the basis of certain procedures of composition: repetition, inversion of phrases, and so on (1300). Needless to say he does not omit to give an analytical presentation of both primary and secondary figures of speech, whether major or minor examples (1302).

2. The West

Here exegetical literature, like all other forms of literature, was in full flower between the end of the 4th and the first decades of the 5th century. But the damage wrought by the barbarian invasions was such as to bring about a rapid, comprehensive, decline though perhaps not uniform, given the regional differences stemming from the break-up of the homogeneous structure of the Empire into the various Romano-barbaric kingdoms.[6] Before moving on to a rapid overview region by region, let us glance at two works of a textbook character, produced in areas which, by this time, had very little connection with each other. They show the widespread demand for this compendium-style of work. This was the preferred resource in overcoming the difficulties of approaching the sacred texts, rather than going directly to the vast commentaries of Jerome, Augustine, or others.

From Eucherius, bishop of Lyon c. 434-455, we have two small treatises: the *Formulae Spiritalis Intelligentiae*, are a collection of words and expressions from Scripture which have some special significance, gathered together by subject-matter (*De supernis creaturis, De terrenis, De interiore homine*, etc.). For each word there is a brief allegorical explanation and then a quotation from Scripture by way of example: 'The eyes of the Lord signify divine supervision, in the sense of the Psalm, the eyes of the Lord are turned towards the virtuous (33:16)'. The *Instructiones* in Bk. I propose in question and answer form the interpretation of passages which are difficult, or at least noteworthy, in the Old Testament and New Testament, following Scripture book by book, with a preference for allegory, though not in any exclusive manner. Book II is a little manual of biblical archaeology and philology: it mentions proper and common names of particular importance, of places, animals, rivers, garments, and so on. Obviously the material in the two books of Eucherius is second hand, as are the principles set out in the introduction to the first treatise: the different senses of Scripture; difficulties of the spiritual sense, which is reserved only for worthy persons; the possibility of overcoming, through adequate explanation, difficulties which can arise from certain anthropomorphisms in the sacred text. Around the middle of the 6th century, the African Junilius dedicated to Primasius the *Instituta Regularia Divinae Legis*, claiming that he had derived them from Paul of Nisibis in the East.

In a clear and precise style, and in question and answer form, the author deals with the number of the sacred books, their authorship, their form, content, and so on. He has interesting criteria for the use of allegory, which ruled almost unopposed in the West, in the period which concerns us here.

If we begin our rapid regional survey in Africa, we might note that almost all the energies of the catholic Church were polarised, during the Vandal domination, by the struggle with Arianism, so that while doctrinal literature was very much to the fore, exegetical output was neglected. The *Liber Promissionum* (also *De Praedictionibus et Promissionibus Dei*) was written, according to popular opinion, by Quodvultdeus, the bishop of Carthage, when he was exiled and took refuge in Campania (439).[7] The work as a whole contains 153 chapters on the promises and predictions made in Scripture, and is designed to show that as the promises of God have been kept in the past, so no-one can doubt that they will continue to be fulfilled till the end of time, which itself is the object of the last predictions. The book is a thesis which attempts to deal with a great quantity of material in a reasonable space, following the encyclopaedic trends of the period. The subject-matter is very traditional in its basic typologies: Adam and Eve are symbols of Christ and the Church, Esau and Jacob are symbols of the Jews and Christians, and so on. This same traditional subject-matter, with a broad preference for allegory either typological or moralising, can be seen in the *Commentarii super Cantica Ecclesiastica* written by Verecundus Iuncensis during the last stages of Vandal domination (c. 520). This is a commentary on nine canticles of the Old Testament (Moses, Deborah, Jeremiah, etc.) which were sung during services. In both these works one can detect echoes of the current situation of the Church, oppressed by the persecution of the Arian barbarians. The *Commentary on the Apocalypse* by Primasius which we mentioned earlier, belongs to the period of Byzantine domination.

Visigoth Spain, even in the flourishing literary period between the end of the 6th and the 7th century, produced exegetical work only in the form of compilations (Isidore, Julian). In the period which concerns us directly (5th to 6th century), we see these tendencies as in the *Commentary on the Song of Songs* by Justus of Urgel (middle of the 6th century) as well as the *Commentary on the Apocalypse* (mentioned earlier) by Apringius of Beja, who was influenced by Tyconius. The former is shaped concisely by traditional christological and ecclesiological interpretation, and develops its basic theme through the variations codified by a long and splendid tradition.

In Gaul too, at the time of the literary high point between the end of the 4th and the early decades of the 5th century, the example of Hilary was not followed and the genre of exegesis was poorly developed: the *Expositio Psalmorum* by Prosper of Aquitaine is merely a summary of Augustine's *Enarrationes on Pss.* 100-150. With all the more reason the genre weakened during the period of decline: we may record the commentaries on Proverbs, Ecclesiastes, Matthew and John attributed to Salonius, the son of Eucherius, because the material, taken from Jerome, Augustine and others, is synthesised in question and answer form, starting a style which was to be popular. There were also such books as the *De Spiritalis Historiae Gestis* by Avitus of Vienne (beginning of the 6th century). These transpositions of episodes in Genesis and Exodus into elegant hexameters testify to the vitality of this particular literary genre in the West, which in the middle of the century would be revived in Rome thanks to the poetic paraphrase of the Acts of the Apostles written and publicly recited with enormous success by Arator. Among the numerous *sermones* of Caesarius of Arles, just a little after Avitus, there is a small number on scriptural subjects. They are of interest to us, not so much for the exegetical method, as for the particular context in which they appeared: I refer to the desperate struggle of Caesarius of Arles against the growing ignorance of his flock, intentionally keeping his preaching at a very low level for the sake of being accessible to the least educated. In such a setting, it is natural that the predominant style of interpretation should be allegorical, whether in a typological or moral sense, in order to bring the biblical text into contact with the experience of the listeners: the Egyptians' persecution of the Jews becomes the persecution of the *populus Christi* by the wicked, the *populus diaboli* (98:2); the call of Abraham is the call of every Christian (81:1ff.). The Gospel passages in particular provide openings for this elementary moral catechesis.

In Italy, dominated by the Goths, the liberal policy of Theodoric encouraged the survival of a certain literary activity which was concentrated in Rome, where the strength of pagan and Christian tradition and the vitality of the senatorial aristocracy maintained a climate which was not closed to cultural development. In this environment, in the period which interests us (and which ends before Gregory the Great) we find that the most noteworthy exegetical work is the *Expositio Psalmorum* by Cassiodorus, even though he wrote it after retiring to the monastery of Vivarium (after 550). In the introduction, the author claims to have intended to abbreviate the voluminous *Enarrationes* of Augustine, but he also used other sources (Origen, Jerome, Cyril) and added his own material. A lengthy introduction considers prophetic inspiration, the Psalms in general and criteria for interpretation. The psalm by psalm commentary shows a competence unusual in works of the kind: there is an introduction, a fairly concise explanation, and a summary conclusion. Given the sources and this form of composition, the exegesis is traditional, mostly allegorical. The intention of the allegory is to highlight the presence of Christ throughout the psalter, using a triple dimension: divine, human and ecclesial (CCL 97, 16). To demonstrate the meanings of the sacred text, which represent the spiritual dimension beyond the literal, Cassiodorus uses traditional exegetical procedures: sometimes the literal interpretation is juxtaposed to the spiritual; sometimes it leads to it, especially in the symbolic value of numbers and on the etymology of Hebrew names. Of particular importance are two external characteristics. One, which we have already mentioned, consists in the systematic and synthetic nature of the commentary, in keeping with the requirements of the day, where the great commentators on the Psalms, Origen and Augustine do not worry about being verbose and lengthy in their treatment. The second consists in the marked grammatical character which Cassiodorus gave to his commentary, literally packed with definitions and observations on syllogisms, etymologies, parables and rhetorical devices of every type. Cassiodorus' work, intended for the use of monks, has the purpose not only of guiding them in their contact with Scripture but also of offering them basic instruction.[8]

With this chapter, we must end the brief outline which we have traced of the history of patristic exegesis of Scripture, by turning out attention to an important passage in John Cassian. In the preceding pages we have shown the extent of the success of Origen's threefold division of the senses of Scripture: literal, spiritual and moral. Cassian, in *Collationes* 14:8, proposes a variation of this division: first he distinguishes *historica interpretatio* from *spiritalis intelligentia*, i.e. the literal from the allegorical interpretation, then he proposes three types of spiritual interpretation: *tropologia, allegoria* and *anagoge*. By *allegoria*, he understands what we have defined as typology,[9] by *anagoge*, he understands the reference from earthly realities to heavenly ones;[10] by *tropologia* he means moral interpretation, *ad emundationem vitae et instructionem pertinens*. We observed the importance for Origen of what Cassian defines as *anagoge* and what he instead called spiritual interpretation and associated with typological interpretation. So the fourfold division of Cassian was derived from Origen's threefold division by splitting Origen's spiritual interpretation into two distinct forms, typological and anagogical.[11]

As far as we know, this is the first instance of a fourfold distinction of the senses of Scripture, rather than three. This distinction, with the others was to prove very popular in mediaeval exegesis.

NOTES

[1.] It is symptomatic that John Philoponus, culturally the most important representative of Alexandria in the first half of the 6th century, was more influenced by Aristotle in his training than by any Christian authors.

[2.] It still found some detractors in the 7th century.

[3.] In the West, Ambrose Autpert (end of the 8th century) was the first to suggest the Marian interpretation.

[4.] And in its entirety only in Latin translation. From the introduction to this book (PG 87, 1, 21) we know the essential features of the larger work.

[5.] Cassiodorus mentions this (*Inst.* 1:10).

[6.] Exegesis was especially cultivated by Irish monks, but only from the 7th century, outside the chronological limits of our historical outline.

7. We are not concerned here with the uncertainties which surround the author of this work – for these, see R. Quasten, *Patrology* IV, London 1981, p. 129.

8. To facilitate the consultation of his work, Cassiodorus included marginal symbols to indicate passages which were important from an exegetical or grammatical point of view.

9. As an example of this type of interpretation, Cassian cites Gal. 4:24 (Hagar and Sarah) from which he also took the term *allegoria*.

10. As an example of *anagogia*, Cassian cites the mention of the Jerusalem above (Gal. 4:26), of which the earthly one is precisely the symbol.

11. Cassian's debt to Origen is underlined by the quotation of Prov. 22:20 *describe ea triplice*, etc. used by Origen to indicate his three scriptural senses. But while Origen refers this passage to the literal sense and two allegorical senses, Cassian refers it to the three allegorical senses.

Appendix

Some Observations on the Theological Interpretation of Scripture in the Patristic Period*

From the very dawn of the Church's life, Scripture has been regarded as a governing tool for all Christian activity, private or community. It immediately assumed a role of quite exceptional importance for defining and preserving the deposit of faith, following the fundamental significance which the Church always attached to this deposit of faith as the very basis and the characterising feature of the true religion of Christ.

In this context, however, both the apostolic message, which gradually crystallised into the writings of the New Testament and even more the Old Testament, presented not an organic system of doctrine, but scattered claims, often linked to a particular occasion and not infrequently difficult to harmonise. For this reason, both the first real doctrinal formulations and successive, gradual developments of doctrine normally came about through argument, debate, and controversy among divergent formulations which resulted in the acceptance of certain doctrines and the condemnation of others (as heresy). And because every proposal had to be based on the authority of some scriptural passage and was often based on several, this particular use of Scripture determined a style of reading and interpretation which had its own distinctive characteristics, compared with the interpretative methods usual in a specifically exegetical setting.

---

* This appendix was first published in *Orpheus* n.s. 2 (1981).

I propose to set out here some considerations on the specific characteristics of this type of scriptural interpretation. However, the scope of this brief essay excludes not only texts of the apostolic and sub-apostolic era, but also those connected with the Gnostic and Marcionite crises in which the Old Testament itself turned out to be one of the main objects of contention, and concentrates (though not exclusively so) on the trinitarian and christological controversies which extended from the second half of the 2nd century to the beginning of the 5th.

In this connection, the first obvious point to make is that the scriptural passages used for doctrinal ends were normally taken out of their original context and considered in isolation, producing results sometimes quite foreign to the sense which they would have had if interpreted within their proper context. Take, e.g., Jn. 4:24: 'God is spirit'. In the setting of the words which Jesus addresses to the Samaritan woman, the expression contrasts the new worship given to God, 'in spirit and in truth', with the older worship which was concretised in sacred places of Jerusalem and Mount Gerizim. But, the word *pneuma* had a whole philosophical (especially Stoic) tradition behind it, so that, taken out of context, it was often used to indicate the divine substance of the Father and the divine element in the Son.[1] When the development of the Arian controversy turned the attention of theologians to the Holy Spirit, the text was then even used to demonstrate the divinity of the third hypostasis of the Trinity.[2]

Precisely because these texts, isolated from their original context, take on a life of their own and are often interpreted in the most diverse ways by different parties in controversy, but always in terms of the new doctrinal and polemical contexts into which they are inserted and which condition their meaning, the hermeneutical procedures which are employed to accommodate them to these new needs entirely abandon the interpretative structures normally used in specifically exegetical settings. Bearing this obvious point in mind, we can see how far off course those scholars are who thought that they could discern a fundamental exegetical component at the root of Arius' doctrine. Because Arius was a disciple of Lucian of Antioch, who was long considered the founder of the exegetical school of Antioch deliberately literalist in opposition to Alexandrian allegorism, it has been suggested that precisely Arius' literal interpretation of key christological and trinitarian texts induced him to formulate his doctrine of the radical subordination, i.e. creatureliness of the Logos in relation to God the Father. Basically he interpreted literally 'The Lord created me...' (Prov. 8:22); 'firstborn of all creation' in Col. 1:15; 'made' in Acts 2:36[3] and similar expressions in other scriptural texts, and deduced from them that the Logos was not begotten in any real sense, but rather created by the Father.[4]

Leaving aside the point that it is unfounded and arbitrary to make Lucian the founder of an Antiochene school of exegesis opposed to the School of Alexandria and limiting ourselves to the exegetical side of the question, it is easy to show that even an allegorist like Origen can at times without difficulty adhere to the literal sense of texts such as Prov. 8:22 and Col. 1:15, and call the Son a 'creature',[5] just as Arius does; but without drawing from this definition the same consequences as Arius. In fact, in Prov. 8:22, Wisdom (i.e. Christ the Logos) is firstly defined as created by God, but then immediately after (v. 25) as 'begotten'[6] by him. Origen, like Justin, Tertullian and others before him gives full value to 'begot me' (v. 25) and considers 'created me' (v. 22) merely as a generic synonym. Arius, on the other hand, completely reverses the order of preference: he takes v. 22 as the primary meaning, and takes 'begot me' of v. 25 as a generic synonym for 'created me', or better, takes it as indicating the special way in which the Father created the Son compared with the rest of creation.[7]

From an exegetical point of view, Arius' procedure is exactly equivalent to that of Origen's; if the direction is opposite and the meaning reversed, it is because in the interpretation of this passage and others in which the Son is defined sometimes as 'begotten' and sometimes as 'created' by the Father, the two start from totally different presuppositions. Origen, though considering the Son to be inferior to the Father, in the tradition of *Logoschristologie*, connects him closely to the Father's divinity and nature and regards him as truly Son. Arius, on the other hand, prefers to underline the immeasurable divide which separates the Father, not only from the rest of creation, but also from the Son and so regards the Son too as a created being, and as Son only in a generic and conventional sense.

This point could be generalised to cover all other biblical passages in which Christ is defined sometimes as begotten and sometimes as created; sometimes as inferior to the Father, sometimes as possessing the same divine prerogatives, texts which Arians and anti-Arians interpreted differently, but using the same exegetical procedure. We should connect the different conclusions, not to differing modes of interpretation (allegorical for the anti-Arians and literal for the Arians) but only to the different theological presuppositions which conditioned the interpretation.[8]

Just the example outlined above shows that when the doctrines held by the opposing parties in a theological debate are duly supported by the authority of at least some scriptural passage, their overall orientation is often determined by more general presuppositions which decisively governed the interpretation of individual passages of Scripture. These presuppositions can stem from the weight of an earlier tradition, from conditions resulting from the development of controversy, from a general view of several scriptural passages, sometimes even from a different philosophical background. On this last point, we can see how authors from the Asiatic environment usually exhibit a materialist type of thought: this is not something deliverately set out, but it is clearly discernible in contrast with the Alexandrian spiritualising tendency with its obvious Platonic origins.[9] Such differing styles of thought often encourage theologians of these two worlds to interpret the same scriptural passages with quite different, even diametrically opposed, results.

For example, Justin, Theophilus and Irenaeus interpret the double account of the creation of man as a repetition of a single creative process and thus identify man created in the image of God in Gen. 1:26 with man formed from the dust of the earth in Gen. 2:7.[10] On the other hand, Origen, following Philo, distinguishes between man made in the image of God and man fashioned from the earth because his Platonic anthropology distinguishes sharply between the spiritual and the bodily component in man.[11] And if Origen criticises the interpretation of his opponents because, if the bodily aspect of man is the image of God, there is a risk that God may be thought to have human features,[12] Ps.-Justin of the *Cohortatio ad Graecos*, considers the Platonic style of interpretation as a hallucination brought about by a crude misunderstanding of the biblical account.[13]

Moving from protology to eschatology, the Asiatic school based their millenarian hopes on a literal interpretation of Rev. 20-21 and various prophetic texts generally taken to have an eschatological meaning.[14] Origen, on the other hand, finds this type of interpretation unacceptably naive, and produces a purely spiritual interpretation for the same texts, obviously using allegorical procedures.[15] Indeed, his spiritualising Platonic outlook, though it did not lead him to the Gnostic excess of denying the resurrection of the body *tout court*, nevertheless did not allow him to envisage such a resurrection as taking place in the definitely corporeal and materialist manner of Asiatic thinking.

We can also add that Col. 1:15 (Christ the image of God) and I Tim. 2:5 (Christ mediator between God and men) are referred in Asiatic circles to Christ as man while in the Alexandrian setting they are referred to Christ as Logos.[16] Even Ps. 109:3: 'From the womb before the dawn I begot you', is sometimes in Asiatic circles referred to the begetting of Christ by Mary, while the Alexandrian School consistently refers the text solely to the divine generation of the Logos.[17] if we return for a moment to Jn. 4:24: 'God is Spirit', we can observe that Tertullian, influenced by Stoic materialism, adduces this text to support his conception of a corporeal, diving spirit, understood as substance shared by the Father and by the Son and of which the latter is only a *portio*, while the Father constitutes the totality.[18] Origen, for his part, systematically interprets Jn.4:24 with the chief aim of excluding the interpretation which we know as Tertullian's,[19] God is spirit, in that he leads us to true life.[20]

* * *

We have said that Scripture does not present a homogeneous corpus of doctrine, but only scattered sporadic traces, indications that are often hard to harmonise. This state of affairs explains why, in the early Christian centuries, quite contradictory doctrines could be set out on the same subject, and yet each would be furnished with suitable scriptural support. The proponents of these theories then had to show not only how and why these given scriptural passages supported their own doctrine, but also and more importantly to interpret the passages produced by their opponents to make them compatible with their own doctrine. To give just a passing example for the time being, Hippolytus and Tertullian, in controversy with the Monarchians, do not limit themselves to supporting their doctrine with Jn. 1:1-3; but have to fit to their own teaching Jn. 10:30 and 14:9-10,[21] texts which their opponents used to support Monarchian doctrine. Sometimes it happened that very important texts were easily turned to provide very different interpretations in support of widely divergent doctrines. To stay with of Jn. 10:30, not only did Hippolytus and Tertullian manage to turn its interpretation against the Monarchians, but during the Arian controversy Asterius, Marcellus and Athanasius all produced very different interpretations.[22] But elsewhere the application of some scriptural passages to one or another teaching was so apt that opponents had to produce an interpretative *tour de force*, or even sometimes resort to escape routes.

The hermeneutical vicissitudes of Scripture passages used in these theological debates were further complicated by the fact that some of them, substantially those which constituted the scriptural foundation for the trinitarian controversies from the 2nd to the 4th century, were called upon with the passage of time and from one controversy after another to give authority to very different and sometimes opposite doctrines. So the texts bounced from one party to the other, always with differing conclusions, through complex sequences of events, sometimes twisted and yet always helping penetrate to the heart of the theological terms of the controversies in question. Obviously, we can only give a few examples to illustrate these exegetical and theological vicissitudes, and will try to choose the most illuminating.

Let us begin with a case which is important not so much for

itself as for the exceptional popularity which a less than plausible interpretation achieved. Jn. 1:3-4: 'All things were made through him, and without him was not anything made. That which was made in him was life'. From the earliest interpretations in the 2nd century (Heraclaeon) until towards the end of the 4th century, without exception, this was interpreted according to the punctuation given above. But when after 360 the Arian controversy turned its attention from the Son to the Holy Spirit, Arians and Pneumatomachians relied on Jn. 1:3 to include the Holy Spirit within all that was created through the Logos[23] thus denying his divine nature. To avoid this interpretation of the text some catholic theologians attached 'that which was made' to the preceding words: 'All things were made through him, and without him was not anything made that was made'[24] so limiting the extent of the creation made through the Son.

Ambrose knew this interpretation, but did not consider it opportune to adopt it; Epiphanius tended to favour it; Chrysostom and Theodore of Mopsuestia[25] accepted it. And while Chrysostom justifies it only for the sake of opposing the Arians, Theodore excludes the traditional interpretation on purely exegetical grounds: he claims indeed, in the apodictic style marks his reading of the sacred text, that the traditional punctuation and interpretation are ridiculous since not all that was made through the Logos was life: the earth, the mountains and many other things besides do not have life. Thus Theodore writes off entire generations of exegetes who had interpreted this passage of John according to the traditional reading, and had understood 'life' in a different and far deeper sense than that taken by the Antiochene.[26] This improbable reading has gradually imposed itself, right up to our own day and has been defended even by exegetes thought to be authoritative.

To turn to passages which have had a much more troubled history in trinitarian debates, let us turn again briefly to Prov. 8:22-25. Justin was the first, as far as we know, to adopt this text, without going into details, to demonstrate the origin of the Logos in God, and the text was taken up in this sense by representatives of 'Logos-theology' as far as Origen and beyond.[27] As we have seen, Arius picked it up from this tradition, but interpreted it in a new way, to show that the Logos was not really begotten, but instead created by the Father. The use which Arius made of the text put his adversaries on the defensive on this point and from then on they struggled to counter the Arian interpretation offering various solutions.

Only rarely was reference made to the Hebrew text which provided a different reading from the Septuagint and so validated Arius' interpretation.[28] Some interpreted 'He created me' in connection with the context: 'at the beginning of his ways, for his works' and took it to mean that God put the Logos over the work of creation and the governing of the world;[29] in the end, however, the interpretation which referred 'created' in v. 22 to Christ's human birth from Mary and 'brought forth' in v. 25 to his divine generation by the Father prevailed.[30] The popularity of an interpretation which to us seems quite arbitrary was due either to the authority of Athanasius, or to a growing tendency among anti-Arian theologians during the 4th century to distinguish clearly the divine qualities in Christ from the human ones. To demonstrate the quandary in which the catholic party found itself when faced with the Arian interpretation of the text, it is enough to recall that Gregory of Nazianzus, albeit only momentarily, wondered whether this 'Wisdom' of Proverbs 8:22ff. ought to be identified with the Logos.[31]

The Gospel of John, given its highly speculative character, was used proportionally more than any other book of Scripture in the trinitarian and christological controversies. Amid the varying debates and changing situations, Jn. 1:1 acquired a relatively stable role, in that it constituted the real strong point for Logos-theologians of the catholic party against their different adversaries. Opposing the Monarchians,[32] they used the text to deduce from 'the Word was with God and the Word was God' the personal subsistence of Christ as God alongside the Father.[33] Later, against the Arians they used it to deduce either the full divinity of the Logos, or (from 'in the beginning was the Word'), his co-eternity with the Father.[34]

Jn. 10:30 ('I and The Father are one'[35]) had a much more chequered history. The Monarchians were first to use it, because the words were easily read in the sense that the Son is completely one with the Father, i.e. is only a mode of his operation in the world.[36] But Hippolytus and Tertullian ably overturned this argument of their opponents: they pointed out that if the neuter ἕν (*unum*) signifies the unity of the Father and the Son, the plural *are* signifies by contrast distinction of persons.[37] In this sense, the text was added to the scriptural dossier of the Logos-theologians, although with varying meanings. Tertullian referred the neuter *unum* to the unity of substance of the two divine persons, while Origen, whom we have already seen to be suspicious towards the idea of a divine substance shared by two persons, prefers to interpret the unity of Father and Son in a dynamic sense, as a unity of will and action.[38] This explanation of Origen's was repeated at the time of the Arian controversy by Asterius the Sophist and by other Arians,[39] but the text was taken up principally by the anti-Arians polemicists who interpreted it in the sense of substantial unity, of the divine nature of the Father and of the Son;[40] in Latin circles, the arguments of Tertullian[41] were taken up again when the need arose.

But the Gospel of John also offered passages which the Arians could easily turn to their own advantage: e.g. Jn. 17:3: 'And this is eternal life, that they know thee the only true God, and Jesus Christ[42] whom thou has sent.' Among such passages, the most telling seems to be Jn. 14:28: 'The Father is greater than I', yet the exegetical and theological life of this passage during the Arian controversy was anything but one-sided, and a rapid review allows us to define the basic aspects of the controversy. First, we should remember that a certain subordinationism was an almost constant feature in trinitarian theology of the 2nd and 3rd centuries, and in this setting the Johannine text was constantly and uniformly cited to show the inferiority of the Son in relation to the Father.[43] The fact that Arius and the first generation of his followers did not use Jn. 14:28, shows precisely that the subordinationism embraced by them was quite different from that of their predecessors. They moved towards more radical statements, until they maintained that the Son is quite extraneous to the nature of the Father, of a different kind in relation to him: the generically subordinating point of Jn. 14:28 was less important in their eyes than such texts as Prov. 8:22; Col. 1:15; and Acts 2:36 from which they believed they could deduce the creatureliness of the Logos.

But the most characteristic aspect of this first phase of the affair is that we find the passage in John used against the Arians. To understand how this came about, we should bear in mind the fact that in this first phase, the anti-Arian party was concerned, not so much with maintaining the total equality of the Son with the Father, as the fact of his belonging to the same substance, the divine nature; and in this sense, Jn. 14:28 could be important in introducing a difference between the Father and the Son which was not qualitative, but only quantitative i.e. one which remained within the limits of the same substance, divine nature.[44] Only with the passage of time, as the catholic party gradually developed its reflections in the direction of the complete equality of the Son with the Father, did their opponents first think to use Jn. 14:28 first against such a development – in the creed produced in 357 at Sirmium, seemingly a compromise, then by Eunomius himself in a more radically Arian way.[45]

With the positions now reversed, the catholics found themselves having to explain the text in a way which would be compatible with their new trinitarian stances. While some extended to this text also the criterion of referring to Christ as man all the characteristics which made him inferior to the Father,[46] others preferred a less banal explanation: the Father is greater than the Son, in that he is his *arche*, the origin from which he derives his divine being[47] Jn. 14:28 represented a case which was somewhat *sui generis*, in that it was put forward in successive period first by one then by the other of the two opposing groups.

More frequently, Scripture passages were given different interpretations by the same group as the controversy over doctrine developed. As usual we will limit our examples to essentials. The theophany of Gen. 18:1ff., which describes the appearance of three men to Abraham by the oak of Mamre, was traditionally interpreted by seeing the three men as the Logos and two angels,[48] an interpretation still attested by Hilary at the height of the Arian controversy (*De Trin.* IV.25, 26, 28). But with the eventual perfection of a global view of the Trinity as three perfectly equal hypostases operating equally in the economy of the world, the passage was given an interpretation in harmony with this definitive trinitarian position and the three men were seen as the three hypostases of the Trinity.[49]

I have been concerned so far with passages involved in the christological/trinitarian controversy, not so much because long study has made me familiar with this field, but because it is easier here, given the variety of the controversies and the length of time they covered, to find examples which suit our purposes. But even in quite different contexts, the same features come into play: suffice it to recall, in the area of soteriology, the very different interpretations given by Augustine to a whole series of Pauline texts in the few years between the *Expositio 84 Propositionum ex Epistola ad Romanos* (394) and the *De Diversis Quaestionibus ad Simplicianum* (396/397), first interpreting them in an anti-Manichaean way to safeguard human free will and then stressing exclusively the gratuitousness of divine aid.[50]

In this same context, it is worth following more widely the range of interpretations given to Matt. 7:17-18 (= Lk. 6:43): 'So every sound tree bears good fruit, but the bad tree bears evil fruit. A sound tree cannot bear evil fruit, nor can a bad tree bear good fruit.' The Gnostics made use of the clear opposition: good tree/good fruit; bad tree/evil fruit, to give a scriptural basis to the central aspect of their doctrine, the dualistic opposition between the good nature and the just nature (and/or wicked).[51] In opposition to this, Tertullian, Origen and other anti-Gnostic polemicists set to work to interpret the text so as to safeguard human freedom, maintaining, as does Origen, that there is only one nature common to human beings who in virtue of their free will become good or bad trees.[52] The Gnostic interpretation was revived by the Manichees, and among the writers who attacked them on this point was Augustine, with an interpretation which tended, like Origen before him, to link the good and bad fruit to human free will.[53] Later, however, Augustine had occasion to return to this text in a very different doctrinal context: i.e. the excessive exaltation of free will by Pelagius. Against Pelagius, who had spoken of a single root (= human nature), which produces good or bad fruit as a result of free will, Augustine resolutely affirms the existence of good and bad trees (i.e. good and bad human beings) stemming from good and bad roots.[54] While Augustine is careful not to follow the Gnostic and Manichaean assertion of two natures,[53] the sense of his argument draws close to such an interpretation, distancing him radically from his own interpretation of the text a few years before in a different controversial setting.

The brief observations which we have set out here are intended only to show how significant, and sometimes tortuous, was the history of the interpretation of certain important Scripture passages involved in doctrinal controversies and so in the development of dogma and how different were the interpretative methods used in these circumstances compared with those normally used in specifically exegetical contexts. If, despite this, if we wish to draw a more general conclusion, it is that even if the patristic age was convinced that the deposit of faith was purely and simply a compendium of scriptural data, in reality the long and varied controversies led to dogmatic definitions far more elaborate than their scriptural starting points. And this process of elaboration of the scriptural data was governed, apart from their intrinsic weight, by a whole series of external factors, ranging from diverse local conditions,[56] to the different way in which theologians of standing (one might think of Augustine) perceived certain fundamental religious needs. In the christological and trinitarian context, much was made of the weight of the *sensus ecclesiae*, i.e. the conviction, deeply rooted in the faithful themselves both of the unity of God, and of the full divinity, together with the full humanity, of Christ.[57] In this regard, it does not seem to be arbitrary to conclude that the final results of the trinitarian and christological controversies in no way detracted from the significance or importance of this basic conviction.[58]

NOTES

[1.] Cf. for example, Tertullian, *Adv. Prax.* 7:8; Athanasius, *De Sententia Dionysii* 15; Ps.-Athan. *Ctr.Apoll.* I 6.

[2.] Cf. Epiphanius, *Ancoratus* 7:70; Basil, *Adv. Eunonium* III 3; *De Spiritu Sancto* 18:47; 19:48.

[3.] Prov. 8:22 (following the Septuagint): 'The Lord created me at the beginning of his ways for his works' (Wisdom in the Old Testament speaking of herself; Christians identify this with Christ the Logos); Col. 1:15 '[the Son] is the image of the invisible God, the first-born of all creation'; Acts 2:36 'God has made him both Lord and Christ, this Jesus whom you crucified'.

[4.] On the exegetical literalism of the Arians, cf. for example, T. E. Pollard 'The Exegesis of Scripture and the Arian Controversy', *Bulletin of the John Rylands Library*, 41 (1959), 417: 'The Arians fell into error, just as Noetus and Praxeas had done before them, because they were too literal in their interpretation of selected texts isolated from their contexts and interpreted, not in the light of the whole teaching of the Bible, but in the light of their own extra-biblical presuppositions.' What Pollard here observes about the Arians, that they isolated Scripture passages from their context, was in fact normal procedure for all early theologians, in spite of occasional claims to the contrary.

[5.] Cf. *De Princ.* IV 4:1; *Comm. in Jo.* I 19 (22); I 34 (39).

[6.] In Prov. 8:25, Wisdom says of herself '(the Lord) brought me forth beyond all the hills'.

[7.] The particular feature of the creation of the Son compared with other creatures was that he alone was directly created by God, while all the others, including the Holy Spirit, were created by the Son through the will of the Father. In interpreting Prov. 8:25 'brought forth' in the sense of 'created me', Arius found a hermeneutical criterion for interpreting similarly those biblical passages traditionally held to indicate the generation of the Logos, e.g. Ps. 109:3.

[8.] We do not possess Arian texts of a specifically exegetical nature dating back to the earliest years of the controversy, to enable us to check whether they were effectively literalist. The *Homilies on the Psalms* written by Asterius the Sophist in later years, when he had distanced himself from the controversy show the co-existence of literalism and allegorism. Very late texts show sometimes an allegorist tendency (*Opus Imperf. in Matthaeum*), at others a literalist tendency (*Commentary on Job*), exactly as one would see in the catholic exegetes of the period. There is really no definite evidence to enable us to claim that the Arians used to interpret Scripture with hermeneutical criteria any different from those used by the catholics.

[9.] For this comparison and its limitations, cf. 'Il Millenarismo in oriente da Origene a Metodio', in *Corona Gratiarum* (Festschrift E. Dekkers), Bruges 1975, p. 40ff.

[10.] Cf. Justin, *Dial.* 62; *De Resurrectione* 7; Theophilus, *Ad Autolycum* I 4; 11, 19; Irenaeus, *Adv. Haer.* IV, praef. 4; A. Orbe, *Antropologia de San Ireneo*, Madrid 1969, pp. 13ff.

[11.] Cf. Origen, *Hom. in Gen.* 1:13. We find the same distinction (again through the influence of Plato) in Gregory of Nyssa, Augustine and other authors of the 4th and 5th century.

[12.] Cf. *Dial. cum Heraclide* 12; *Sel. in Gen.*, PG 12, 93, where Origen specifies that the Asiatic Melito deduced from this type of interpretation of the Genesis story that God is incorporeal.

[13.] Cf. Ps.-Justin, *Cohort.* 29-30. The unknown author directly criticises Plato, accusing him of having distinguished two creations by misunderstanding the

Genesis account, but it is not impossible that by 'Plato' he meant the Christian Platonists of Alexandria.

[14.] In presenting a picture of the millennium on the basis of prophetic passages from the Old and New Testaments, Irenaeus several times explicitly claims, in opposition to the Gnostics, that those passages cannot be interpreted allegorically (*Adv. Haer.* V 35, 1:2).

[15.] Cf. *De Princ.* II 11:2, 3. Even if Origen did not specifically have Irenaeus in mind, the contrast between the two positions emerges clearly.

[16.] Cf. Irenaeus, *Demonstr.* 22; *Adv. Haer.* V 17:1; Tertullian, *Adv. Marc.* V 19, 3; *De Carne Christi.* 15:1; Origen, *De Princ.* I 2, 5, 6, 7; II 6:1.

[17.] Justin, *Dial.* 63, 83; Ps.-Hippolytus, *In Sanctum Pascha,* 3:2;. Tertullian, *Adv. Marc.* V 9:7, 8. We have said that this interpretation occurs sometimes in authors in Asiatic circles, because they also generally interpret Ps. 109:3 as a reference to the divine generation of the Logos, like the Alexandrians. On all of this, see the careful observations of G. Otranto, *Esegesi biblica e storia in Giustino,* Bari, 1979, p. 43ff.

[18.] Cf. *Adv. Prax.* 7:8, 8:4, 9:2.

[19.] Cf. *De Princ.* I 1:1, 2; *Comm. in Jo.* XIII 21-23.

[20.] Cf. *De Princ.* I 1:4; *Comm. in Jo.* Origen here interprets this passage in John's Gospel by relating it to the totality of the context in which it is situated.

[21.] Jn. 10:30. 'I and the Father are one'; Jn. 14:9-10. 'He who has seen me has seen the Father . . . Do you not believe that I am in the Father and the Father in in me?'

[22.] We will deal specifically with these different interpretations, when we examine these particular passages in John shortly.

[23.] This interpretation of Jn. 1:3 had already been anticipated by Origen, who nevertheless cites it with great caution: *Comm. in Jo.* II 10(6).

[24.] This punctuation 'that was made' connects with 'all things were made through him' and 'without him was not anything made' becomes an incidental expression.

[25.] Ambrose, *Expositio Ps.* 36:35; Epiphanius, *Panarion* 69:56; John Chrysostom, *Hom. in Jo.* 5:2; Theodore of Mopsuestia, *Comm. in Jo.* CSCO 116, 17. For greater detail on this subject, cf. K. Aland, 'Eine Untersuchung zu Joh. 1, 3. 4', *ZNW* 59 (1968), 190ff.

[26.] I.e. in the sense of spiritual life, according to the interpretation of Heracleon, Origen and others.

[27.] The first author who uses Prov. 8:22ff. to demonstrate that the generation of the Logos, who is the Wisdom and the Power of God precedes the creation of the world, is Justin (*Dial.* 61). In this doctrinal context, some later theologians adapt the passage to provide more precise meanings: e.g. Tertullian (*Adv. Prax.* 7:1-3), cites this passage along with others to illustrate the idea that the Logos from eternity and impersonally within God, had been begotten by him at a second stage as a distinct person for the purpose of the creation of the world. Origen, who refuses to distinguish two separate stages in the God/Logos relationship uses the present tense in Prov. 8:25 ('I *am* brought forth') to sustain his position that the generation of the Son by the Father must be understood as eternal and continuous, i.e. eternally present (*Hom. in Jer.* 9:4).

[28.] Indeed the Hebrew *qanah,* which the Septuagint had here translated as *ektise,* has a much wider significance, and the other Greek translators of the Old

Testament rendered it as *ektesato* ('the Lord possessed me', etc.); Eusebius of Caesarea holds to this version in *De Eccl. Theologica* III 2, followed later by Basil (*Adv. Eunomium* II 20).

[29.]See for example, Hilary, *De Trin.* XII 38.

[30.]We first encounter this interpretation in its complete form in Athanasius (*S. Arianos* 2:44ff.). Earlier, Marcellus of Ancyra had interpreted both verse 22 and verse 25, by applying them to the birth of Jesus from Mary, in keeping with his doctrine which does not consider the Logos, but only as the one born of Mary to be the Son of God in a real sense (fr. 11:12, 27 and passim). Also a fragment from Eustathius of Antioch (60) applies Prov. 8:22 to the incarnation of the Logos. Complications similar to those which developed around Prov. 8:22 can be seen also for Col. 1:15: 'First-born of all creation'. In fact before the Arian crisis this expression had been applied to the Logos (cf. for example Tertullian, *Adv. Prax.* 7:1; Origen, *De Princ.* I 2:1) as begotten by the Father. Following the Arian interpretation, which exploited the text to view the Logos not as begotten, but as created, the passage was no longer taken by the catholic party to refer to divine generation: Athanasius and Hilary, for example, apply the text to the creative activity of the Logos (Athanasius, *C. Arianos* 2, 62, 63, 64; Hilary, *De Trin.* VIII 50).

[31.]*Orat.* 30:2. Even if Gregory of Nazianzus, who reports this doubt as having been advanced by others, finishes by repeating the interpretation of Athanasius (cf. n. 30). However, the very fact that there was doubt surrounding the identification of Wisdom in Prov. 8:22 with the Logos, signifies the embarrassing situation in which the catholics found themselves in relation to the Arian interpretation, because as we have seen the interpretation was already current in the 2nd century and no-one had previously thought of questioning it.

[32.]The term is understood here only in reference to the Patripassians and the Sabellians, i.e. the Monarchians whom modern scholars term modalist.

[33.]Cf. Hippolytus, *C. Noetum.* 14; Tertullian, *Adv. Prax.* 13:3.

[34.]In connection with this it is sufficient to recall Hom. 16 of Basil, entirely concerned with expounding Jn. 1:1 against the Arians and also the Sabellians.

[35.]This text was normally paired with Jn. 14: 9-10. We consider it here by itself only for the sake of brevity.

[36.]Cf. Hippolytus, *C. Noetum* 7; Tertullian, *Adv. Prax.* 20:1-2.

[37.]Hippolytus, *C. Noetum* 7; Tertullian, *Adv. Prax.* 22:10-11. Before he develops this argument, Tertullian observes (20, 2) that it is a good rule to interpret *pauciora* by starting with *plura* and throughout chap. 21, he produces a long series of passages, starting with Jn. 1:1-3, which confirm his teaching in opposition to the Monarchians.

[38.]For Tertullian cf. the texts cited in n. 18 and 37; for Origen cf. *C. Celsum* VIII 12; *Comm. in Jo.* XIII 36; *Comm. in Cont.*, Prologue, p. 69 (GCS, Baehrens).

[39.]Cf. Asterius fr. 32, Bardy; *Frag. Arr.* 4, PL 13, 602.

[40.]Cf. for example, Athanasius, *C. Arianos* 3:3, 4, 5.

[41.]Cf. Hilary, *De Trin.* VII 25; Faustius, *De Trin.* 12 (CCL 69, 305). A similar episode to that of Jn. 10:30 and 14:9-10 was that of Bar. 3:36-38 ('This is our God, no other can be reckoned beside him . . . he appeared upon earth and lived among men') and Is. 45:14 ('They will make their prayers to you because God is in you, and they will say, "There is no God besides you" '). The passages were taken up by the

Monarchians, because they could emphasise the identification of the Son with the Father (Hippolytus, *C. Noetum* 2); but Hippolytus and Tertullian had interpreted them so as to underline the distinction of the Son from the Father (Hippolytus. *C. Noetum* 4:5; Tertullian, *Adv. Prax.* 13:2; 16:3). In this interpretation the two texts were taken up differently in opposition to the Arians, because both could easily be used to underline the unity of nature of the Son with the Father (Athanasius, *Serap.* 2:4; Hilary, *De Trin.* IV 38-40, 42; V 39).

[42.]Cf. Hilary, *De Trin.* IV 8 (the passage is echoed by Arius at the beginning of the letter to Alexander, p. 12, Opitz). The catholic party responded by underlining the clear association which the text establishes between Christ and the Father: Athanasius, *C. Arianos* 2:81; Hilary, *De Trin.* III 14.

[43.]Cf. for example Tertullian, *Adv. Prax.* 9:2; Origen, *C. Celsum* VIII 14; *Comm. in Jo.* XIII 25; Irenaeus, *Adv. Haer.* II 28:8. The example of Irenaeus is particularly representative of the general diffusion of the concept, given the author's deliberate abstention from trinitarian speculation.

[44.]Cf. Alexander, *Epistola ad Alexandrum Thess.*, p. 27f., Opitz; Athanasius, *C. Arianos* 1:58. The reasoning is based on the presupposition that only homogeneous and not heterogeneous quantities can be compared: one can compare a man with a man, but not a man with a horse, as was observed in an argument by the author of Ps.-Basilianus *C. Eunonium*, PG. 29, 693.

[45.]Cf. Hahn, *Bibliothek der Symbole*, p. 200f.; Eunomius, *Apol.* 11.

[46.]Ps.-Athanasius, *Sermo maior de fide*, p. 10, Schwartz; Ambrose, *De Fide* II 8:59; IV 12:168; Augustine, *De Trin.* I 7:14.

[47.]Cf. Basil, *Adv. Eunonium* I 25; Epiphanius, *Panarion* 69:53. Hilary grounds both interpretations, explaining that the Father is greater than the Son, in his relationship of origin and that the latter is inferior by reason of the human form which he assumed. *De Trin.* XI 51ff.

[48.]Cf. Origen, *Hom. in Gen.* 4:1.

[49.]Ps.-Didymus, *Trin.* II, PG 39, 628f.; Ambrose, *Spir.* II, *prol.* 4; Augustine *De Trin.* II 11:20. In the same way, Old Testament passages which insist on the uniqueness of God, e.g. Deut. 6:4, Is. 44:6, which the Arians produced to support the claim that only the Father is the supreme God, and which Hilary endeavoured to explain by saying that the mention of the Father includes also the Son (*De Trin.* IV 33) were later explained as referring to the whole of the Trinity: Gregory of Nyssa, *Quod Non Sint Tres Dei* p. 42, Muller; *C. Eunonium.* III 3:110, Jager; Ambrose *De fide* I 1:6.

[50.]Cf. *Expos.* 60, 62; *Ad Simplicianum* I 2, 3, 7, 9, 12, 15, on Rom. 9:10-13, 15-21 etc.

[51.]Cf. Tertullian, *Adv. Marc.* I 2:1; *De Anima* 21:4; Origen, *De Princ.* I 8:2; II 5:4.

[52.]Cf. Tertullian, *De Anima* 21:4-5; Origen, *De Princ.* II 5:4; *Comm. in Rom.* III 6; VIII 11.

[53.]Cf. *C. Fortunatum Manichaeum* I 14:15; *De Actis cum Felice Manichaeo* II 2, 4.

[54.]Cf. *De Gratia Christi* I 18, 19.

[55.]He denies that he wishes to propose the concept of a nature *ab origine* intrinsically evil.

[56.]One can think, for example, of the influence exercised by Greek philosophy, an influence which took various forms depending both on the different Christian environment (Stoicism was more favoured in Asia in the 2nd century, Platonism more in Alexandria in the 3rd century), and also especially on the varying fortunes of the different schools: the flourishing Christian Platonism of the 3rd and 4th centuries which was so much in evidence in the development of trinitarian and christological doctrine, was directly related to a flourishing of pagan Platonism; and the emergence of Aristotelianism in the 5th century christological controversies corresponds to a similar popularity of Aristotle in the pagan world.

[57.] This ecclesial *sensus* found support also in the fact that the catholic theologians were time after time able to back up their doctrines with many more biblical passages than their adversaries. We have already mentioned (cf. n. 37) Tertullian's observation that it is necessary to interpret *pauciora* on the basis of *plura*; and in the Arian controversy the accumulation of biblical passages against heretics was characteristic of Athanasius and other catholic polemicists; suffice it to recall here Gregory of Nazianzus' spectacular presentation of passages which demonstrated the divinity of the Holy Spirit (*Orat.* 31:29).

[58.] The patristic material which I have used here, at times in rather compendious form, to illustrate these brief notes, has been at least partly dealt with more analytically in my previous works. For greater detail I suggest the following: *Studi sull'arianesimo*, Rome 1965; 'Note di cristologia pneumatica', *Augustinianum* 12 (1972) 201-232; *La crisi ariana nel IV secolo*, Rome 1975; 'Matteo 7, 17-18 dagli gnostici ad Agostino', *Augustinianum* 16 (1976) 271-290; 'Giovanni 14.28 nella controversia ariana', in *Kyriakon* (Festschrift J. Quasten), Münster n.d. pp. 151-161.

Bibliography

No attempt has been made to provide a comprehensive
bibliography, although some items have been added for this
English edition, especially from among the numerous
publications which have appeared since the original Italian
edition. For further bibliography, and for a fuller treatment of
many of the subjects discussed in this work, see especially M.
Simonetti, *Lettera e/o allegoria: un contributo alla storia dell'esegesi
patristica,* Rome 1985.
   For editions and translations of patristic works referred to,
the reader should consult B. Altaner, *Patrology* (Freiburg 1960),
and J. Quasten, *Patrology* in 3 vols. (Utrecht 1950-1957), with
additional volume ed. by A. de Berardino (Turin 1970; English
translation, Westminster, Maryland 1986).

G. Bardy, 'Commentaires patristiques de la Bible', *Dictionnaire de
la Bible* Supplément II, 75-103; Id.,' Exégèse patristique', *ibid.* IV,
569-591 (s.v. 'Interprétation'); Id., 'La littérature patristique des
Quaestiones et Responsiones sur l'Ecriture Sainte', *Revue biblique*
41 (1932) -42 (1933); *La Bible et les Pères. Colloque de Strasbourg,*
Paris 1971; *Biblia patristica,* Paris 1975ff. (index of Biblical
quotations used by the Fathers, so far four volumes have been
published for the period to the 4th century); *The Cambridge
History of the Bible* I, Cambridge 1970; H. Crouzel, 'La distinction
de la "typologie" et de l' "allégorie"', *Bulletin de littérature
ecclésiastique* 65 (1964) 161-174; J. Daniélou, *Sacramentum futuri,*
Paris 1950; *Les symboles chrétiens primitifs,* Paris 1961; *Études
d'exégèse judéo-chrétienne (Les Testimonia),* Paris 1966; Id., *A History
of Early Christian Doctrine before the Council of Nicaea,* I-III (London
and Philadelphia, 1964-77); R. M. Grant, *The Letter and the Spirit,*
London 1957; J. C. Joosen and J. H. Waszink, 'Allegorese',
Reallexikon für Antike und Christentum I, 283-293; H. de Lubac,
'"Typologie" et "allégorisme"', *Recherches de science religieuse* 34

(1947) 180-226; Id., 'Sens spirituel', *ibid.* 36 (1949) 542-576; Id., 'À propos de l'allégorie chrétienne', *ibid.* 47 (1959) 5-43; Id., *Exégèse médiévale* I, Paris 1959; B. de Margerie, *Introduction à l'histoire de l'exégèse.* I. *Les Pères grecs et orientaux*, Paris 1980; IV. *L'Occident Latin*, Paris 1990. G. T. Armstrong, *Die Genesis in der alten Kirche*, Tübingen 1962; E. Dassmann, *Der Stachel im Fleisch. Paulus in der frühchristlichen Literatur bis Irenaeus*, Münster 1979; R. Devreesse, *Les anciens commentateurs grecs de l'Octateuque et des Rois*, Vatican City 1959; Id., *Les anciens commentateurs grecs des Psaumes*, *ibid.* 1970; C. Diestel, *Geschichte des Alten Testaments in der christlichen Kirche*, Jena 1869 (repr. Leipzig 1980); Y. M. Duval, *Le livre de Jonas dans la littérature chrétienne grecque et latine*, Paris 1973; J. Gamberoni, *Die Auslegung des Buches Tobias in der griechisch-lateinischen Kirche der Antike und der Christenheit des Westens bis um 1600*, München 1969; R. A. Greer, *The Captain of Our Salvation. A Study in the Patristic Exegesis of Hebrews*, Tübingen 1973; A. Lindemann, *Paulus im ältesten Christentum*, Tübingen 1979; H. Merkel, *Die Widersprüche zwischen den Evangelien. Ihre polemische und apologetische Behandlung in der Alten Kirche bis zu Augustin*, Tübingen 1971; F. Ohly, *Hohelied-Studien*, Wiesbaden 1958; K. H. Schelkle, *Paulus Lehrer der Väter*, Düsseldorf 1956 (Rom.); P. Siniscalco, *Mito e storia della salvezza. Ricerche sulle più antiche interpretazioni di alcune parabole evangeliche*, Turin 1971; N. B. Stonehouse, *The Apocalypse in the Ancient Church*, Goes 1929; M. F. Wiles, *The Divine Apostle*, Cambridge 1967 (Paul). Id., *The Spiritual Gospel*, Cambridge 1960 (John); E. Corsini, *Apocalisse prima e dopo*, Torino 1980.

Chapter 1

§1. O. Betz, *Offenbarung und Schriftforschung in der Qumransekte*, Tübingen 1960: R. Bloch, 'Midrash', *Dictionnaire de la Bible Supplément* V, 1253-1280; A. Díez Macho, *El Targum. Introducción a las traducciones aramaicas de la Biblia*, Barcelona 1972 (with bibl.); L. Ginzberg, *The Legends of the Jews* I-VII, Philadelphia [12]1968; D. Patte, *Early Jewish Hermeneutic in Palestine*, Missoula 1975; E. Schürer, *The History of the Jewish People in the Age of Jesus Christ* II, Edinburgh [2]1979, pp. 314-380 (with bibl.);

G. Vermes, *Scripture and Tradition in Judaism,* Leiden ²1973; J. Pépin, *Mythe et allegorie,* Paris ²1976.

Philo: E. Bréhier, *Les idées philosophiques et religieuses de Philon d'Alexandrie,* Paris ²1925; I. Christiansen, *Die Technik der allegorischen Auslegungswissenschaft bei Philo von Alexandrien,* Tübingen 1969; I. Heinemann, *Philos griechische und jüdische Bildung,* Breslau 1932 (repr. Hildesheim 1973); P. Heinisch, *Der Einfluss Philos auf die älteste christliche Exegese,* Münster 1908; V. Nikiprowetzky, *Le commentaire de l'Écriture chez Philon d'Alexandrie,* Leiden 1977; C. Siegfried, *Philo von Alexandria als Ausleger des Alten Testaments,* Jena 1875 (repr. Aalen 1970).

§2. New Testament: J. Bonsirven, *Exégèse rabbinique et exégèse paulinienne,* Paris 1939; C. H. Dodd, *According to the Scriptures,* London 1952; E. E. Ellis, *Paul's Use of the Old Testament,* Edinburgh 1957; R. H. Gundry, *The Use of the Old Testament in St Matthew's Gospel,* Leiden 1967; J. R. Harris and V. Burch, *Testimonies* I-II, Cambridge 1916-1920; B. Lindars, *New Testament Apologetics,* London 1961; O. Michel, *Paulus und seine Bibel,* Gütersloh 1929 (repr. Darmstadt 1972); G. Reim, *Studien zum alttestamentlichen Hintergrund des Johannesevangeliums,* Cambridge 1974; F. Schroger, *Der Verfasser des Hebräerbriefes als Schriftausleger,* Regensburg 1968; K. Stendahl, *The School of Matthew,* Lund ²1967; F. C. Synge, *Hebrews and the Scriptures,* London 1959.

The Apostolic Fathers: L. W. Barnard, *Studies in the Apostolic Fathers and their Background,* Oxford 1966; K. Beyschlag, *Clemens Romanus und der Frühkatholizsmus,* Tübingen 1966, pp. 48-134; J. Klevinghaus, *Die theologische Stellung der Apostolischen Väter zur alttestamentlichen Offenbarung,* Gütersloh 1948; P. Prigent, *Les testimonia dans le christianisme primitif. L'Epître de Barnabé I-XVI et ses sources,* Paris 1961; K. Wengst, *Tradition und Theologie des Barnabasbriefs,* Berlin 1971.

§3. The Gnostics: C. Barth, *Die Interpretation des Neuen Testaments in der valentinianischen Gnosis,* Leipzig 1911; A. Orbe, *Estudios Valentinianos* I-V, Rome 1958-1966; M. Simonetti, 'Note sull'interpretazione gnostica dell'Antico Testamento', *Vetera Christianorum* 9 (1972) 331-359; 10 (1973) 103-126; R. McL. Wilson, 'The Gnostic and the Old Testament', in *Proceedings of the International Colloquium on Gnosticism*, Stockholm 1977, pp. 174-198.

§4. Justin: L. W. Barnard, *Justin Martyr*, Cambridge 1966; B. Kominiak, *The Theophanies of the Old Testament in the Writings of St Justin*, Washington 1948; G. Otranto, *Esegesi biblica e storia in Giustino (Dial. 63-84)*, Bari 1979 (with bibl.); P. Prigent, *Justin et l'Ancien Testament*, Paris 1964; W. A. Shotwell, *The Biblical Exegesis of Justin Martyr*, London 1965.

Tertullian: J. E. L. van der Geest, *Le Christ et l'Ancien Testament chez Tertullien*, Nijmegen 1972 (with bibl.); T. P. O'Malley, *Tertullian and the Bible*, Nijmegen 1967; J. H. Waszink, 'Tertullian's Principles and Methods of Exegesis', in *Early Christian Literature and the Classical Intellectual Tradition*, Paris 1979, pp. 17-31; G. Zimmermann, *Die hermeneutischen Prinzipien Tertullians*, Würzburg 1937.

Irenaeus: S. Herrera, *S. Irénée exégète*, Paris 1920; J. Hoh, *Die Lehre des hl. Irenäus über das Neue Testament*, Münster 1919; J. T. Nielsen, *Adam and Christ in the Theology of Irenaeus*, Assen 1968; A. Orbe, *Parábolas evangélicas en san Ireneo* I-II, Madrid 1972. M. Simonetti, 'La sacra Scrittura in Teofilo d'Antiochia', in *Epektasis, Mélanges J. Daniélou*, Paris 1972, pp. 197-207.

§5. Hippolytus: *Ricerche su Ippolito*, Rome 1977.

Chapter 2

§1. Clement: J. Daniélou, 'Typologie et allégorie chez Clément d'Alexandrie', in *Studia patristica* IV, Berlin 1961, pp. 50-57; A. Méhat, 'Clement d'Alexandrie et les sens de l'Écriture', in *Epektasis, Mélanges J. Daniélou*, Paris 1972, pp. 355-365; C. Mondésert, *Clément d'Alexandrie*, Paris 1944; R. Mortley, *Connaissance religieuse et herméneutique chez Clément d'Alexandrie*, Leiden 1973.

§2. Origen: R. Gögler, *Zur Theologie des biblischen Wortes bei Origenes*,

Düsseldorf 1963; R. P. C. Hanson, *Allegory and Event*, London 1959; N. R. M. de Lange, *Origen and the Jews*, Cambridge 1976; H. de Lubac, *Histoire et Esprit*, Paris 1950; V. Peri, 'Criteri di critica semantica dell'esegesi origeniana', *Augustinianum* 15 (1975) 5-27.

Chapter 3

§1. Eusebius: D. S. Wallace-Hadrill, *Eusebius of Caesarea*, London 1960, pp. 59-99.

§2. and 4. The School of Antioch: J. Guillet, 'Les exégèses d' Alexandrie et d'Antioche, conflit ou malentendu?', *Recherches de science religieuse* 34 (1947) 257-302; Ch. Schäublin, *Untersuchungen zu Methode und Herkunft der antiochenischen Exegese*, Bonn 1974; P. Ternant, 'La theoria d'Antioche dans le cadre des sens de l'Écriture', *Biblica* 34 (1953) 135-158, 354-383, 456-486; A. Vaccari, 'La "theoria" nella scuola esegetica d'Antiochia', *Biblica* 1 (1920) 3-36; Id., 'La "teoria" esegetica antiochena', *ibid.* 15 (1934) 94-101. L. Leloir, *Doctrines et méthodes de S.Ephrem d'après son commentaire de l'Évangile concordant*, Louvain 1961.

Diodorus: E. Schweizer, 'Diodor von Tarsus als Exeget', *Zeitschrift für die neutestamentliche Wissenschaft* (1941) 33-75; M. J. Rondeau, 'Le Commentaire des Psaumes de Diodore de Tarse et l'exégèse antique du Psaume 109/110', *Revue de l'histoire des religions* 176 (1969) 5-33, 153-188.

Theodore of Mopsuestia: R. Devreesse, *Essai sur Théodore de Mopsueste*, Vatican City 1948; R. A. Greer, *Theodore of Mopsuestia, Exegete and Theologian*, London 1961; L. Pirot, *L'oeuvre exégétique de Théodore de Mopsueste*, Rome 1913; M. Simonetti, 'Note sull'esegesi veterotestamentaria di Teodoro di Mopsuestia', *Vetera christianorum* 14 (1977) 69-102; U. Wickert, *Studien zu den Pauluskommentaren Theodors von Mopsuestia*, Berlin 1962.

John Chrysostom: R. Kaczynski, *Das Wort Gottes in Liturgie und Alltag der Gemeinden des Johannes Chrysostomus*, Freiburg 1974; A. Merzagora,' Giovanni Crisostomo commentore di S. Paolo', *Didaskaleion* n.s. 9 (1931) 1-73.

Theodoret: G. W. Ashby, *Theodoret of Cyrrhus as Exegete of the Old Testament*, Grahamstown 1972.

§3. The Cappadocians: P. Scazzoso, 'San Basilio e la Sacra Scrittura', *Aevum* 47 (1973) 210-24. M. Harl (ed.), *Ecriture et culture philosophique dans la pensée de Grégoire de Nysse*, Leiden 1971.

§4. Didymus: W. A. Bienert, *Allegoria und Anagoge bei Didymos dem Blinden von Alexandria*, Berlin 1972; J. Tigcheler, *Didyme l'Aveugle et l'exégèse allégorique*, Nijmegen 1977.

Cyril: A. Kerrigan, *St Cyril of Alexandria Interpreter of the Old Testament*, Rome 1952; M. Simonetti,' Note sul commento di Cirillo ai Profeti minori', *Vetera christianorum* 14 (1977) 301-330; R. L. Wilken, *Judaism and the Early Christian Mind: A Study of Cyril of Alexandria's Exegesis and Theology*, London 1971.

Chapter 4

§1. Cyprian: M. A. Fahey, *Cyprian and the Bible*, Tübingen 1971.

Hilary: N. J. Gastaldi, *Hilario de Poitiers exegeta del Salterio*, Paris 1969; Ch. Kannegiesser,' L'exégèse d'Hilaire', in *Hilaire et son temps*, Paris 1969, pp. 127-142.

Ambrose: G. Lazzati, *Il valore letterario dell'esegesi ambrosiana*, Milano 1960; E. Lucchesi, *L'usage de Philon dans l'oeuvre exégétique de saint Ambroise*, Leiden 1977; H. auf der Maur, *Das Psalmenverständnis des Ambrosius von Mailand*, Leiden 1977; L. F. Pizzolato, *La dottrina esegetica di sant'Ambrogio*, Milan 1978; H. Savon, *Saint Ambroise devant l'exégèse de Philon le Juif*, Paris 1977.

§2. A. Souter, *The Earliest Latin Commentaries on the Epistles of Paul*, Oxford 1927; W. Erdt, *Marius Victorinus Afer, der Lateinische Pauluskommentator*, Bern 1979.

§3. Jerome: J. Braverman, *Jerome's Commentary on Daniel*, Washington 1978; W. Hagemann, *Wort als Begegnug mit Christus: Die christozentrische Schriftauslegung des Kirchenvaters Hieronymus*, Trier 1970; A. Penna, *Principi e caratteri dell'esegesi di s. Gerolamo*, Rome 1950.

§4. Augustine: C. Basevi, *San Agustín: La interpretación del Nuevo Testamento*, Pamplona 1977 (with bibl.); M. Comeau, *Saint Augustine exégète du Quatrième Evangile*, Paris 1930; U. Duchrow, *Sprachverständnis und biblisches Hören bei Augustin*, Tübingen 1965; A.M. La Bonnardière, *Biblia augustiniana*, Paris 1963ff.; G. Pelland, *Cinq études de saint Augustin sur le début de la Génèse*, Paris-Montréal 1972; M. Pontet, *L'exégèse de saint Augustin prédicateur*, Paris 1945; G. Strauss, *Schriftgebrauch, Schriftauslegung und Schriftbeweis bei Augustin*, Tübingen 1959.

Chapter 5

A. Ceresa-Gastaldo, 'Contenuto e metodo dell'Expositio psalmorum di Cassiodoro', *Vetera christianorum* 5 (1968) 61-71; C. Curti, 'Spiritalis intelligentia: Nota sulla dottrina esegetica di Eucherio di Lione', in *Kerygma und Logos: Festschrift C. Andresen*, Göttingen 1978; R. Devreesse, 'Chaines exégétiques grecque', *Dictionnaire de la Bible* Supplément I, 1114-1139; S. Gennaro, 'Infussi di scrittori greci nel Commento all'Ecclesiaste di S. Gregorio di Agrigento', *Miscellanea di studi di letteratura cristiana antica* 3 (1951) 162-184; U. Hahner, *Cassiodors Psalmenkommentar*, München 1973; H. S. Hoskier, *The Complete Commentary of Oecumenius on the Apocalypse*, Ann Arbor 1928; G. Langgärtner, 'Der Apokalypse-Kommentar des Caesarius von Arles', *Theologie und Glaube* 57 (1967) 210-225; G. Mercati, 'Pro Adriano', *Revue biblique* n.s. 11 (1914) 246-255; R. Schlieben, *Christliche Theologie und Philologie in der Spätantike: Die schulwissenschaftliche Methode der Psalmenexegese Cassiodors*, Berlin 1974.

Scripture Index

General Index